HEALTH CARE IN TRANSITION

MANAGERIAL SOLUTIONS TO HOSPITALS' CHALLENGES

HEALTH CARE IN TRANSITION

Additional books in this series can be found on Nova's website
under the Series tab.

Additional e-books in this series can be found on Nova's website
under the eBooks tab.

HEALTH CARE IN TRANSITION

MANAGERIAL SOLUTIONS TO HOSPITALS' CHALLENGES

FEDERICA MORANDI, PHD

nova publishers
New York

Library of Congress Cataloging-in-Publication Data

ISBN: 978-1-63484-784-1
Library of Congress Control Number: 2016933383

Published by Nova Science Publishers, Inc. † New York

Questo libro è dedicato a Emma che è vera gioia di vivere!

CONTENTS

PREFACE

In the attempt to provide a global vision of the challenges faced by hospitals, this book analyzes the dense network of rules and expectations coming from institutions, patients and professionals in which healthcare organizations are embedded.

The numerous changes that have occurred within a large part of the healthcare systems during the last 20 years, have determined important consequences, which have been promptly faced by managers. Uncertainty, rules, and innovations are just some of the main ingredients of the challenges to be tackled, whereas mimicry, legitimacy and diffusion of managerial fashions are some of the core strategies implemented to face them. Hospitals survival depends on the ability to intercept on time and to accomplish quickly the external expectations. The role of managers is to create a workplace in which changes are possible. Individual and organizational work value congruence can facilitate it by improving the quality of communication, the degree of trust in hospitals' missions, and physicians' and nurses' knowledge of the processes. Hospital challenges reach up to the single physician, often asking him/her to play new and conflicting roles. The "new" physician needs to balance his/her time to accomplish ambiguous expectations, to fulfill heterogeneous tasks, and to compete for scarce resources in order to embrace the changes. In this vein, physicians' negotiation skills assume a strategic role for the successful running of hospitals.

ACKNOWLEDGMENTS

I wrote this book on the basis of my deep attraction for the hospitals. Even before starting my studies on healthcare organizations, I was really fascinated about their complexity. The different colors of the uniforms, the shifts rotations, the communication with patients and their relatives, the operating rooms rules represent just some of the striking themes.

I was not so brave to become a physician (!) and so I decided to be involved into the healthcare organizations by providing my contribution to the study about the organizational design and the people management of hospitals. The person who brightened my studies that I really want to thank is Professor Americo Cicchetti. During the second year of the Bachelor Degree in Management of Healthcare organizations at Catholic University, I attended his course about the organization of the hospitals. It was an amazing experience, which determined my future decisions. Later I had the opportunity to work for some months at the "Policlinico Gemelli" hospital, in which I was employed into the Hospital Admissions Center. Here I understood how the expectations of patients, the professionals' skills and the organizations rules are strictly connected. And here I decided to go deep into the study of hospitals. At the end of the Academic degree I was admitted to the Ph.D. program in Management of healthcare organizations, and during this period I had the opportunity to learn more on theories and evidence about healthcare organizations challenges. Professor Cicchetti gave me the possibility to attend national and international workshops and conferences and to be involved into national research programs. Because of this, I came in contact with the hospitals environment, I visited many healthcare organizations, meeting many Hospitals CEOs and Departmental Directors. During the same years thanks to my colleague Prof. Daniele Mascia, who is one of the more skilled and patient person who I know, I had the opportunity to start to be involved into the academic debate through the publication of scientific papers.

When I had the opportunity to write this monograph I thought to all the things that I could have said about healthcare organizations. But the more interesting topic was the analysis of some of their major challenges, related to both external and internal rules and expectations. During the draft of the monograph I received the help of many people who provided me support and suggestions. Firstly Professor Joseph Gonnella, who read the preliminary version of the monograph and who gave me important advices. Thanks to my colleagues Domenico Addesso and Luca Giorgio who helped me in the data collection. To Luca Giorgio, Irene Gabutti and Marco Rizzo, thank you for the helpful friendly review of the book chapters. Another important reviewer is my father Roberto, who reviewed the chapter 5. To him and to my mother Gloria thank you for always believing in me and in my skills, but also for all the helps and opportunities you gave and give me. Thanks to my brother Matteo who continuously keeps me calm! And finally a special thanks to the most important parts of my life: my husband Germano, who encourages and loves me, and our wonderful Emma, who is our masterpiece!

Chapter 1

INTRODUCING HOSPITAL CHALLENGES

ABSTRACT

Healthcare managers need to be aware of the daily challenges the hospitals they lead, face. The ability to tackle them effectively is strategic for organizational success. Particularly, knowing the sources of challenge takes on strategic value. Challenges may come from the environment, which imposes rules and expectations, but also from the internal sources of an organization. The ability to fulfill external requirements is a tactical move to guarantee the organization's survival. Moreover, the talent to handle the need to standardize, together with the capacity to attribute decisive power to employees is necessary to reach good levels of performance within the workplace. Contextually, the aptitude to intercept and fulfill employees' values increases the possibility to rely on satisfied physicians and nurses. Due to their fundamental role in the process of care, the challenges emerging from organizational behavior need to be in turn considered.

There are multiple possibilities to manage hospital challenges which need a systematic and punctual activity of analysis.

Keywords: hospital challenges, structural dimensions, contextual dimensions, clinical directorate

INTRODUCTION

The introduction of the main sources of challenge for hospitals represents the principle aim of the present chapter. In particular we want to demonstrate that the high complexity characterizing healthcare organizations[1], implies frequent changes, and determines the variation of the employees' needs and behaviors. Moreover, healthcare organizations are subjected to several rules and various expectations which appear to be stronger, than those affecting organizations in other contexts.

A series of tools and definitions are supplied throughout the chapter in order to explain the evidence provided later on.

The first source of challenge can be recognized inside the organization when considering the role of structural and contextual dimensions. For instance, under specific conditions the organizational culture, the level of formalization and the decentralization of power become a challenge. Additionally, we provide a description of the context in which Italian hospitals operate that is a further source of challenge.

Furthermore, the relationships that hospitals maintain both internally and externally play a significant role for their survival. Healthcare organizations need to interact and to cooperate with different external bodies such as institutions, customers, competitors, in order to survive and to exchange goods and resources. In this vein according to the contingency theory, an organization must adapt to the characteristics of its context to survive and to be effective [1]. The consideration of the organizational context is essential in finding the correct fit between the structure and its environment, and thus making the organization run more efficiently [2-7]. According to the contingency theory [8-11], the fit between organizations and their environment is the result of natural selection forces. In other words, the distribution of resources in the environment determines the structure of organizations. In any case, both the old approaches to the contingency theory and recent ones strongly recognize the role of environmental forces and the external expectations and rules in the surviving organization. Based on the above-mentioned considerations, in chapter two we analyze the challenges emerging from institutional pressures, which compel hospitals to adopt ceremonial behaviors to accomplish them.

In chapter three, we describe the phenomenon of social contagion among organizations, as well as the diffusion of managerial fads and fashions. We are convinced about the strength with which external forces, coming from

[1]We will use the terms hospitals and healthcare organizations as synonymous. In our opinion, both of them can be used as general terms to describe organizations, in which care to patients is provided. Healthcare organizations refer to different institutional typologies of hospitals, which in the Italian healthcare context are characterized by a heterogeneous model of governance and different goals.

institutions and opinion leaders, shape healthcare organizations. In addition, the central role of individuals is essential both within knowledge-based organizations, and healthcare [12], in which physicians and nurses provide core activities i.e., patient care. Their good performance depends on their skills but also on their motivation, satisfaction and commitment to the organization they work for.

Chapter four shows, that the "*value of the values alignment*" [13] is essential to create an appreciable workplace. Therefore, the challenge faced by hospitals is also represented by the employees' behavior and their ability to accept new roles and tasks. For that reason, chapter five is dedicated to the ability of physicians to negotiate internally and externally. Starting from an analysis of the main changes which have occurred within healthcare organizations, following the introduction of the New Public Management principles, chapter five illustrates how physicians' work has been modified by the assumption of administrative roles along with clinical ones. The balance between the two roles assigned to physicians, implies the development of various negotiating abilities. In particular, the internal negotiation concerns physicians' ability to strike a balance between clinical and administrative activities. The aptitude for exploiting negotiating skills in carrying out the new administrative tasks and during budget discussions, characterizes the external negotiation.

Rules and Expectations Affecting Healthcare Organizations

Healthcare organizations operate within a highly institutionalized context in which the rules imposed by the external bodies, together with the external expectations, affect all managerial decisions. Healthcare organizations are considered extremely hard to manage and to design because of the double nature of the pressures to which they are subjected, technical and institutional [14]. The technical dimension concerns the production systems sphere and the resources useful to produce. Moreover, it involves all the factors able to influence demand, such as, the socio-demographic characteristics of customers and the competitors' features. On the other hand, the institutional environment describes the "group of cultural-cognitive knowledge" named norms, coming from the legal environment and the regulation systems, which give sense and stability in a specific field [15]. Many authors [16, 17] affirmed that organizations operating in highly institutionalized environments are more likely to survive if they are able to observe the norms, thus obtaining legitimacy. In order to be coherent with the external requests, healthcare organizations are prone to mime the successful experiences achieved by other organizations [14, 15]. For example, within the US healthcare system, Ruef and Scott [14] documented that institutional bodies, such as the Joint Commission on the Accreditation of Healthcare Organizations (JCAHO) or the American Medical Association (AMA), confer legitimacy by reviewing the structures and functions of healthcare organizations and certifying the quality of their processes. Awareness of the coexistence of the technical and the institutional dimensions leads to more comprehensible choices and behaviors within the organizations. In particular, organizations operating in highly technical environments are evaluated and rewarded based on their effective productivity. They need to focus their attention on the coordination and the control of technical processes. On the contrary, organizations operating in highly institutionalized contexts, such as healthcare, need to take into consideration the efficiency and the effectiveness of their activities together with institutional pressures. The complexity of healthcare organizations consists in a twofold task: being constantly efficient and respecting external rules and expectations.

Designing the Organization: Looking at the Structural and the Contextual Dimensions

According to literature two groups of dimensions characterize an organization: structural and contextual ones [18]. The structural dimensions indicate centralization, formalization, hierarchy, specialization and training, in a general perspective, they affect the internal specific traits of an organization. Contextual dimensions, which indicate the general features of an organization are the environment, the mission and strategy, the size, the level of technology and the organizational culture.

Environment: The environment indicates the nature of external influences and activities in the political, technical, social and economic arenas. The environment in which the organizations operate can be divided into two levels: the specific environment and the general environment. The specific environment indicates all the external influences and relationships that characterize a given organization (its customers, its suppliers, its competitors).

The general environment, on the other hand, indicates the influence and relationships that affect organizations playing in the same political or economic arena. The uncertainty generated by the external expectations and requests is crucial for healthcare organizations, which can even decide to decouple their external shape from their internal core activities, thus indulging the institutional pressures (chapter two). For the same reason managers may decide to observe and imitate successful experiences, thus stimulating innovations diffusion (chapter three).

Mission and strategy. The mission of an organization is its unique overall priority and desired end-state. The strategy is the way by which managers decide to operate in order to reach the organizational mission. Generally, managers decide to adopt a strategy based on their own knowledge and competencies. Often, within highly institutionalized contexts, the strategies are adopted taking into consideration the institutional pressures (chapter two), rather than the managerial fads and fashions regarding the adoption of specific organizational models or processes (chapter three).

Size. It represents the bulk of an organization. Usually, it is measured as the number of people and resources employed within the organization. In our context it plays a significant role in the decision to adopt innovations. As demonstrated in chapter three, larger hospitals have more physicians than small ones and as a consequence, they share a richer network of contacts with other professionals. It allows them to capture and to report new practices to their organizations. On the other hand, smaller hospitals are more flexible and prone to introduce innovations. For example, when an innovation requires a modification to performing activities, the smaller the hospital the lower the resistance to introduce changes. It is because they are faster than large organizations in the implementation of innovations.

Technology. It indicates how the organizational goals are reached. The choice to introduce a specific kind of technology depends on the nature of the activities, the specialization, and the types of equipment and facilities needed. Woodward [2] provides a large number of implications coming from the complexity of the technology employed, which are associated with the level of training of the employees, rather than managerial control. Within healthcare organizations the level of technology employed may be highly complex, and therefore needs to be considered during the process of certification, described in chapter three.

Culture. Organizational culture needs particular attention because it permeates the whole organization. The decision whether or not to introduce an innovation, the adoption of external rules, but also the quality and the efficacy of communication patterns within the organizations are strictly related to culture [19]. *Culture* refers to the values and beliefs shared by all organizational members. The employees' attire, slogans or organizational tales about myths and events represent cultural manifestations. Within healthcare organizations the coexistence of different "cultures" of physicians, nurses and administrative staff, makes creating collaborations between them difficult. For that reason, we are convinced that an understanding of the organizational culture is fundamental to interpret both organizational events and managerial decisions.

The structural dimensions are:

- *Centralization:* the level of centralization concerns the extent to which managers decide to spread or to concentrate the decisional power along the hierarchical chain. In particular, when the decisions are concentrated at the corporate level of the organization, the power is centralized. On the contrary, if the power is attributed to all organizational members, the level of centralization is low, and the power is decentralized. Centralization is an extremely significant feature that will be explored in the text in order to examine the consequences of the introduction of the New Public Management principles in the healthcare context (chapter five). The increased level of physicians' autonomy led to a consequent major level of decentralization of power. The clinical directorate model, which is one of the results of the New Public Management principles application, provides a clear example of it.
- *Formalization:* indicates the level of policies and procedures characterizing the organization. The higher the level of formalization, the higher the attempts to maintain the variability of the activities within physiological limits. The need to formalize derives from the size of an organization. Due to the amount of processes and people that need to be coordinated, large organizations need high levels of formalization. However, it also depends on the typology of the performed activities. When the heterogeneity of the achievable results is high, it is necessary to introduce a certain amount of formalization of both procedures and processes by using standards. As we will see in chapter three, standards help the good management of the organization, and their use is crucial when considering the high variability of the results characterizing healthcare service.

- *Hierarchy*: the degree of hierarchy describes the span of control within the organization. The typical trade-off is between hierarchical organizational structures, in which there are numerous managerial levels, following a pyramid layout, or flat organizations in which there are few or no levels of management between the corporate and staff level employees. In modern organizations, the need for flexibility leads to the design of flat organizations and it determines certain implications in terms of human resource management. Those implications are mainly related to the employees' need to experiment job satisfaction, in terms of values cohesion between the individual and the organization. For instance, flat organizations cannot provide vertical career progression, thus making the introduction of alternatives necessary to satisfy the employees extrinsic work values, such as, economic progression based on the broad banding system [20].
- *Specialization*. The degree of specialization indicates the extent to which activities are horizontally divided among employees. The higher is the level of specialization the higher is the focus on one specific task. Furthermore, the level of specialization is progressively increasing within healthcare organizations, thus creating difficulties in terms of coordination around the patient's bed. As chapter four shows, it is possible to face them through the achievement of a common pattern of communication based on value sharing.
- *Training*: It concerns the level of knowledge and skills achieved by the employees, on which the daily activities of the organization are based. Within healthcare organizations the training of physicians is a lengthy process, especially for some medical specializations, and consequently it generates high appreciation for the status and the prestige work values, as illustrated in chapter four.

The analysis of both the contextual and structural features of organizations helps us to interpret the evidence provided throughout the monograph. The dimensions pointed out by Daft [18] are visible within each kind of organization, but they assume a different relevance in correspondence to different contexts. For instance, within healthcare organizations the role of the environment and the size of the organization are both responsible for important variations in terms of ability to introduce innovations. Structural dimensions have a similar strategic role.

The Italian National Health System and the Institutional Typologies of Hospitals

The Italian NHS (I-NHS) was established in 1978 and it provides universal coverage through a single payer system, following the British NHS model. In the early 1990s, the I-NHS took initial steps to introduce new organizational models aimed at improving quality and efficiency in service provision. Healthcare restructuring introduced a quasi-market institutional framework, stimulating competition among public providers and it corporatized hospital organizations by increasing their level of autonomy and accountability [21]. In 1999 the Italian Ministry of Health set into motion legislative intervention that regulated the internal organizational model of Italian hospitals [22], introducing the clinical directorate model. The clinical directorate model (see following paragraph), was a major change for the Italian healthcare system. In fact, it represents a common ground for all institutional typologies of hospitals compelled by law to introduce this new organizational arrangement.

Healthcare institutions worldwide are characterized by a wide variety of hospital typologies [23]. They show substantial differences in terms of objectives, services provision, model of governance and organizational structures. For example, Catholic hospitals in the United States manifest objectives and organizational models that are significantly different from those of other typologies of hospitals [24]. Teaching or research hospitals also have unique characteristics that modify the activities and working conditions of their employees, and in some cases these modifications are substantial [25, 26].

Italian hospitals are classified into four main institutional categories, which are similar with respect to their legal form, ownership structure, institutional objectives, and types of services provided. Hospital Trusts are public hospitals that provide highly specialized (tertiary) care and are characterized by high levels of entrepreneurial autonomy. LHUs' Hospitals are publicly owned organizations and are responsible for providing community healthcare. Hospital Teaching Trusts are linked to universities and provide highly specialized care. Finally National Institutes for Scientific Research are research-oriented hospitals that provide a limited number of highly specialized services [27].

Italian hospitals present some commonalities which allow us to consider the various institutional profiles as part of a unique system.

- Within the Italian system, *health* is one of the fundamental rights guaranteed by the Constitutional Charter. The provision of care to all citizens, independently of their geographical location, religion, gender and economic condition, is the responsibility of each hospital operating on behalf of the Italian NHS;
- Italian public hospitals guarantee the continuity of care. This means that in order to provide the most appropriate care: if a patient needs acute care, at first he/she will be admitted to a Trust Hospital, but later during the rehabilitation phase, he/she will be admitted to a LHU's hospital;
- In Italy care provision is without borders. A patient may decide to be admitted to a given hospital without any geographical constraints and without taking into account the institutional profile;
- Although the regionalization of care, starting from the 90's more autonomy in the healthcare sector has been offered to Italian Regions, while the general conditions regarding the minimum level of assistance provided by Italian hospitals are centrally decided by the Italian Ministry of Health;
- Most Italian hospitals have adopted the clinical directorates [28], indifferently from their institutional profile. The adoption of a common organizational arrangement allows them to reach similar objectives, and to use analogous managerial approaches. Further information on the clinical directorate model is given below.

Despite the existing differences in terms of intensity of care provided, the Italian healthcare organizations may count on general principles, which make them part of the same panorama. Nevertheless, the results provided in the following chapters will be discussed taking into consideration the main features of each institutional profile.

In order to provide an additional clarifying element, the next paragraph is dedicated to the analysis of the clinical directorate model and its strategic role within Italian hospitals.

THE CLINICAL DIRECTORATE MODEL

Clinical directorates represent semiautonomous hospital divisional units in which several clinical wards are integrated or merged [29], considering their level of homogeneity to pursue common care goals. As business models, they are specifically created for resource management, control, and accountability [30, 31]. Clinical directorates have been introduced worldwide based on the recognition of their power to achieve several goals, such as improving the quality of care and also the general efficiency of services [30, 32-34]. The clinical directorate model was implemented for the first time during the 1960s by teaching hospitals in the United States. The aim was to integrate highly specialized skills while exploiting economies of scale and scope through a constant sharing of costly resources [35]. In the Italian NHS, clinical directorates were introduced during the 90s'. Their aim was to reorient the activities toward healthcare processes through the use of organizational units overseeing strategic and organizational decisions [28, 30]. The Italian Ministry of Health has repeatedly stressed the importance of the clinical directorate as a new managerial model for NHS hospitals. The clinical directorate has been considered the most suitable model to balance the need for greater efficiency with quality improvement. A first Legislative Decree (502/92) introduced clinical directorates with the aim to reorganize emergency care within public hospitals. Some years later, a nationwide reform (Legislative Decree 229/1999) recommended the clinical directorate as the best model to organize hospital care, compelling all Italian hospitals to adopt the new arrangement [30]. By adopting the clinical directorate model, hospitals achieved the necessary legitimacy by obtaining formal accreditation by the I-NHS. The national legislative framework regulated some organizational design aspects of the clinical directorates by establishing the new role of clinical director and several departmental collegial representative bodies [27]. Regional authorities contributed to the regulation of directorates with the introduction of additional guidelines aimed at favoring an effective implementation at the local level. Despite this central and regional regulation, many aspects concerning organizational design of the new arrangement were not regulated and rested in the hands of hospital executives, who were free to decide how to implement the new model within their organizations [30, 22].

Literature shows different types and models of directorates related to the criteria used to merge clinical wards into departments [28, 30]. In particular, it is possible to recognize two specific criteria [30, 33]: the "Specialty integration" criterion by which hospital wards are grouped based on medical specialties (e.g., directorate of surgery). In this case, as Braithwaite and colleagues [36] note, the clinical directorate is "*rationally derived from the pre-existing organization of medicine.*" The second distinction, the so-called "Process-integration" (or divisional design) criterion, encouraged preexisting hospital ward units to be grouped based on specific patient conditions (e.g., directorate of cancer). In this case ward units are grouped together with regard to specific body parts or organs, as well as patient age. In addition to the two criteria described above, Italian hospitals created clinical directorates according to a third criterion: "Mixed-integration" [27]. The result of using this criterion is the creation of a departmental structure in which both the Specialty-integration and Process-integration logics coexist [27, 28]. The adoption of one criterion over another appears to be extremely important for internal processes and expected outcomes within hospitals [30, 31, 33, 37]. For instance, when hospital wards are grouped based on similarities among professionals, the possibility to increase clinical knowledge or the possibility to exploit economies of scale increases, thus positively affecting organizational efficiency. In contrast, the Process-integration criterion exerts a strong impact on patient treatment and continuity of care within hospital settings. The grouping of heterogeneous clinical specialties and technological resources within directorates allows multidisciplinary interactions [33, 27].

Besides the managerial and clinical implications, clinical directorates exerted an impact on the behavioral sphere of both physicians and nurses. Firstly clinical directorates affected their sense of belonging. Before the clinical directorates implementation, nurses and physicians could not compare their values within a defined group, thus creating informal and unknown sub-groups. The clinical directorates allow healthcare employees to know who their colleagues are, thus increasing the possibilities of value sharing and values alignment.

A second behavioral implication is represented by the new roles attributed to physicians. Generally, physician job satisfaction increases in relation to organizational modifications in which the sustained psychological costs, induced by the changes, are outweighed by the benefits resulting from the innovation. [38]. Moreover, a positive employee predisposition and commitment is contingent upon the existing fit between structural characteristics of newly adopted arrangements and the personal traits of individuals who are involved in the reorganization [39]. With the introduction of the clinical directorate model, physicians started to be involved in new managerial tasks besides their main clinical activity.

Chapter five focuses on the analysis of physicians' perception of their new double role, and in particular, their negotiating skills.

CONCLUSION

In the attempt to shed light on the challenges faced by the hospitals, this chapter provides useful elements for the debate. Both external and internal sources of challenge are examined. The difference between the technical and institutional environment leads to a discussion about the parameters on which an organization's evaluation is based. The aim is to demonstrate that hospitals are more difficult to manage than other organizations, due to their need to perform in both technical and institutional environments. When considering the internal based challenges, each dimension was illustrated, in order to offer food for thought and elements for an adequate appreciation of the evidence provided. We supplied general information on the Italian NHS and on all the institutional profiles of the hospitals operating on its behalf, as a part of a unique system. Finally, the main features of the clinical directorate model were illustrated, it being the most widespread organizational model within Italian healthcare organizations.

REFERENCES

[1] Van de Ven Andrew H., and Robert Drazin. 1985. "The concept of fit in contingency." Discussion Paper, Strategic Management Research, Center University of Minnesota.

[2] Woodward, Joan. 1958. *Management and Technology*. London: HMSO.

[3] Pugh, Derek S., David J. Hickson, and Robert C. Hinings. 1969. "An empirical taxonomy of Structures of Work Organizations," *Administrative Science Quarterly*, 14: 115-126.

[4] Child, John. 1973. "Predicting and Understanding Organization Structure," *Administrative Science Quarterly*, 18: 168-185.

[5] Burns, Tom. E., and George M. Stalker. 1961. *The Management of Innovation*. University of Illinois: Urbana-Champaign's Academy for Entrepreneurial Leadership Historical Research Reference in Entrepreneurship.

[6] Emery, Fred E., and Eric Trist. 1965. "Causal texture of organizational environments." *Human Relation*, 18: 21-32.
[7] Chandler, Alfred. 1962. *Strategy and structure*. Cambridge, MA: M.I.T. Press.
[8] Hannan, Michael T., and John Freeman. 1977. "Population Ecology of Organization," *American Journal of Sociology*, 82 (5).
[9] Comstock, Donald. E. and Laura S. Schroger. 1979. "Hospital Services and Community Characteristics: The Physician as Meditator." *Journal of Health and Social Behavior*, 20: 89-97.
[10] Aldrich, Howard E. 1979. *Organizations and environments*. Englewood Cliffs, NJ: Prentice-Hall.
[11] McKelvey Bill. 1982. *Organizational systematics: Taxonomy, evolution, classification*. Berkeley, CA: UC Press.
[12] Mascia Daniele, Silvia Dello Russo, and Federica Morandi. 2015. "Exploring Professionals' Motivation to Lead: A Cross-level Study in the Healthcare Sector." *International Journal of Human Resource Management*, 26(12): 1622-1644.
[13] Edwards, Jeffrey R., and Daniel M. Cable. 2009. "The Value of Value Congruence." *Journal of Applied Psychology*. 94(3): 654-677.
[14] Ruef, Martin and Richard Scott. 1998. "A multidimensional model of organizational legitimacy: hospital survival in changing institutional environments." *Administrative science quarterly*, 43(4): 877-904.
[15] Scott, Richard W., Martin Ruef., Peter J. Mendel and Carol A. Caronna. 2000. *Institutional Change and Healthcare Organizations. From Professional Dominance to Managed Care*. The University of Chicago Press: London.
[16] Scott, Richard W., and John W. Meyer. 1983. *Organizational environments: ritual and rationality*. CA Sage, Beverly Hills.
[17] Baum, Joel A.C., and Oliver C. 1992. "Institutional Embeddedness and the Dynamics of Organizational Populations." *American Sociological Review*. 57 (4): 540-559.
[18] Daft Richard L. 1992. *Organizational Theory and Design*. West Publishing, St. Paul, Minnesota.
[19] Danison, Daniel R., and Aneil K. Mishra. 1995. "Toward a theory of organizational culture and effectiveness." *Organization science*, 6 (2): 204-223.
[20] Arnold Edwin W., and Clyde J. Scott. 2002. "Does broad banding improve pay system effectiveness?" *Southern Business Review*, 27 (2).

[21] Anessi Pessina, Eugenio and Elena Cantu`. 2006. "Whither managerialism in the Italian National Health Service?." *International Journal of Health Planning and Management*, 21: 327-355.

[22] LoScalzo, Alessandra, Andrea Donatini, Letizia Orzella, Americo Cicchetti, Silvia Profili, and Anna Maresso.2009. "Health care system in transition: Italy health system review." *Health Systems in Transition*, 11, 1-21.

[23] World Health Organization, 2012. *Modern health care delivery systems, care coordination and the role of hospitals*. World health organization, European Office.

[24] White, Kenneth R., James W. Begun and Wenqiang Tian. 2006. "Hospital Service Offerings: Does Catholic Ownership Matter?" *Health Care Management Review*, 31: 99-108.

[25] Pizzo, Philip A. 2008. "Case Study: The Stanford University School of Medicine and Its Teaching Hospitals." *Academic Medicine*, 83: 867-872.

[26] Ovseiko, Pavel V., Axel Heitmueller, Pauline Allen, Stephen M. Davies, Glenn Wells, Gary A. Ford, Ara Darzi, and Alastair M Buchan. 2014. "Improving accountability through alignment: the role of academic health science centers and networks in England." *BMC Health services research*, 14: 24.

[27] Mascia, Daniele, Federica Morandi, and Americo Cicchetti. 2014. "Looking Good or Doing Better? Patterns of Decoupling in the Implementation of Clinical Directorates." *Health Care Management Review*, 39(2): 111-123.

[28] Cicchetti, Americo, Alessandro Ghirardini, Daniele Mascia, Federica Morandi, Anna Ceccarelli, Vincenzo Vigiliano, Piera Poletti, Rosetta Cardone, Giuseppe Murolo. 2009. "Il modello organizzativo dipartimentale nel Ssn: risultati dell'indagine nazionale." *Politiche Sanitarie*, 10(3): 153-168. (peer-reviewed).

[29] Mintzberg, Henry. (1979). *The structuring of organizations*. Englewood Cliffs, N.J.: Prentice-Hall.

[30] Lega, Federico. 2008. "The rise and fall(Acy) of clinical directorates in Italy." *Health Policy*; 85:252–62.

[31] Braithwaite, Jeffrey. 2006. "An empirical assessment of social structural and cultural changes in clinical directorates." *Health Care Analysis*;14:185–93.

[32] Braithwaite, Jeffrey, Mary T. Westbrook, Rick A. Iedema, Nadine A. Mallock, Rowena Forsyth, Kai Zhang. 2005. "A tale of two hospitals:

Assessing cultural landscapes and compositions." *Social Science and Medicine*, 60: 1149-1162.

[33] Braithwaite, Jeffrey, Mary T. Westbrook, Don Hindle, Rick A. Iedema, and Daniel A. Black. 2006. "Does restructuring hospitals result in greater efficiency. An empirical test using diachronic data." *Health Services Management Research*, 19: 1-12.

[34] McNulty, Terry, and Ewan Ferlie. 2004. "Process transformation: Limitations to radical organizational change within public service organizations." *Organization Studies*, 25: 1389-1412.

[35] Dunnion, Mary, and Elizabeth Dunne. 2004. "Clinical directorates: Stakeholders' knowledge and expectations." *British Journal of Health Care Management*, 10, 10-17.

[36] Braithwaite, Jeffrey, Terence Finnegan, Elizabeth Graham, Pieter Degeling, Don Hindle, and Mary Westbrook. 2004. "How important are safety and quality for clinical-managers? Evidence from triangulated studies." *Clinical Governance*; 9: 34–41.

[37] Cicchetti Americo. 2004. *La progettazione organizzativa*. Milano: Franco Angeli [in Italian].

[38] Caldwell, Steven D., and Yi Liu. 2011. "Further investigating the influence of personality in employee response to organizational change: the moderating role of change-related factors." *Human Resource Management Journal*; 21:74–89.

[39] Caldwell Steven D., David M. Herold, and Donald B. Fedor, 2004. "Towards an understanding of the relationships between organizational change, individual differences, and changes in person-environment fit: a cross-level study." *Journal of Applied Psychology*, 89:868–82.

Chapter 2

THE CEREMONIAL APPROACH OF HEALTHCARE ORGANIZATIONS: A SURVIVING CHALLENGE

ABSTRACT

In order to understand how organizations struggle to survive in their context, this chapter analyzes the main theories on the ceremonial approach of organizations with a particular focus on healthcare organization conduct. Drawing on the neo-institutional theory according to which organizations tend to appear legitimate to external stakeholders chapter two analyzes how this legitimizing process takes place. Especially when the context is uncertain, organizations tend to mime, or bend to external expectations adopting the most appropriate designs or procedures to obtain external legitimacy. Often this adoption is just a formal arrangement due to the organizational decoupling between internal activities and external shape. The decoupling phenomenon affects healthcare organizations creating consequences for institutional stakeholders, managers, professionals and patients, as shown subsequently.

Keywords: decoupling, institutional pressures, legitimacy

INTRODUCTION

For a long time the interest of organizational design scholars has been focused on how organizations face uncertainty in an attempt to survive. In the last decades many authors have recognized an increasing role of the external context in the life of organizations. The anti-managerial theory [1] recognized that the conduct of organizations needs to be aligned with external context expectations [2, 3], especially when they operate in strongly institutionalized sectors, in which external appreciation is a source of survival.

Drawing on institutional theory this chapter analyzes how managers deal with organizational activities and structures, to allow the organizations they lead to keep operating and growing. Generally managers try to adopt organizational models, procedures and practices which are characterized by a low risk of failure. They are more prone to adopt solutions emerging from the mimicry of successful organizations or adopting law propositions or the suggestions of professionals instead of following their own ideas. As a result organizational models appear progressively very similar to each other thereby causing a decrease of the innovation rate in whole sectors.

A further important consideration is that in several contexts, and notably in healthcare, it is possible to perceive that the expected changes appear to be just formally adopted. This opportunistic behavior generates significant consequences, for instance the "patients cream skimming" exerted by hospital managers and professionals in order to appear more efficient. A further example is the adoption but not the consequent implementation of organizational models in the attempt to look more coherent with legal prescriptions.

In order to analyze all these open questions this chapter is organized as follows: the first section is focused on the analysis of institutional theory interpreted as the organizational attempt to balance efficiency and legitimacy. The analysis is then particularly focused on the healthcare context and on how institutional pressures determine the similarity between healthcare organizations. The second section is dedicated to the institutional pressures relief, analyzing a theoretical approach regarding the decoupling phenomenon. This paragraph is followed by a literature analysis of decoupling experienced in the healthcare sector which provides insight into whether healthcare organizations are decoupling. The last section is dedicated to the analysis of decoupling phenomenon consequences, followed by the general conclusions.

Institutional Theory and Organizational Challenges: Balancing Efficiency and Legitimacy

Organizational studies are trying to find an answer to the questions about how and why organizations decide to adopt new organizational models or perform new practices and activities, or finally, why organizations are interested in obtaining external certifications. Traditionally scholars identified two major competing solutions to these questions [4, 5]. The first one considers organizations as rational participants, able to identify and to implement organizational designs, practices and activities in line with the external context needs [6, 7]. In this vein the decision of the organizations to exchange goods, services and resources with other organizations, or the decision to adopt new organizational models seems to be only based on the study of the market conditions in terms of supply and rational demand.

The second perspective affirms that "*organizations require more than material resources and technical information if they want to survive and thrive in their social environment*" [8, 9]. This perspective, known as the neo-institutionalism approach [10, 3, 2], pays more attention to the institutional environment, rather than the technical one. The institutional environment represents the social construct in which organizations work and perform. It represents a challenge for organizations operating in contexts such as healthcare, or education, which are not judged on the basis of their efficiency and efficacy, but rather on their ability to fulfill institutional rules and the external expectations of customers and decision makers [11-15, 2]. Therefore organizational activities seem to focus more on legitimacy than on efficiency [16].

The different approaches implemented by organizations operating in low institutionalized contexts and high institutionalized ones are represented in Figure 1. The first graph represents the linear approach in which the organizational strategy is based: the study of the market conditions and customer preferences. The second graph, on the other hand, shows a more complex and circular approach, which needs to be implemented within high institutionalized contexts. The graph shows clearly that the sources of change are represented by both institutional stakeholders and customers. In the graph the internal pressure exerted by professionals operating within healthcare organizations is not yet contemplated, and is the cause of important organizational conducts, as the decoupling phenomenon (for the definition of *decoupling* see below).

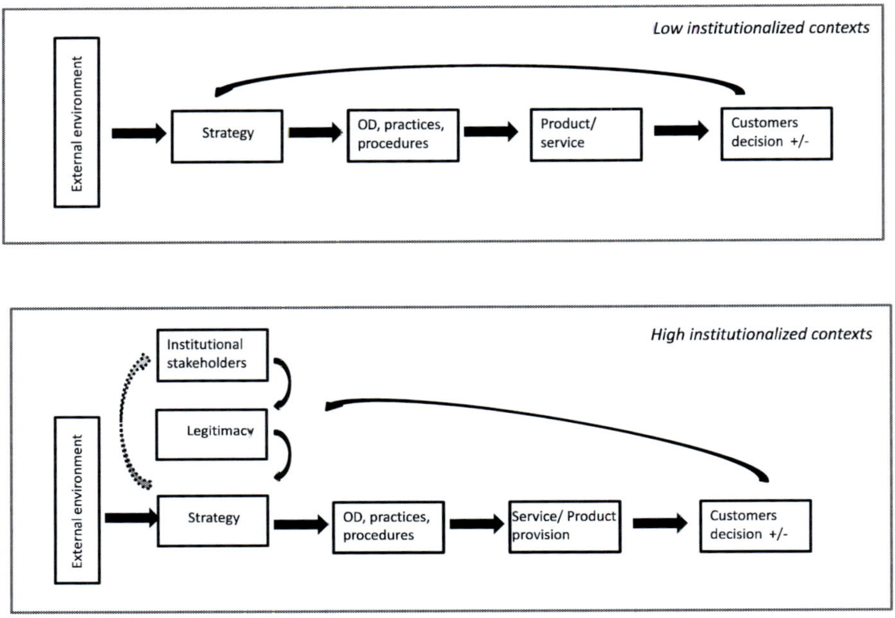

Figure 1. Conceptual differences between low institutionalized and high institutionalized contexts.

One of the peculiarities which emerges in the second graph is the role of legitimacy. Legitimacy represents the extent to which an organization is perceived as desirable, proper and appropriate by a certain social sector [17-19] from which the resources derive. For that reason low legitimized organizations risk jeopardizing their survival because of their general difficulties in obtaining capital, labor, and partners.

In the Deephouse [20] definition, legitimacy is considered "*a status conferred by social actors,*" and in this perspective a legitimate organization is the one "*whose values and actions are congruent with that social actor's values and expectations for action.*" This means that it is not necessary that the decisions implemented by the organization appear useful, but it is fundamental that they be congruent with social expectations.

Organizations endowed with legitimacy are in a favored position. In this vein the contribution of Deephouse [20] suggests that organizations adopting the same strategies as other successful organizations, obtain more endorsement compared to those that deviate from legitimate behavior. Similarly, organizations that are able to gain external legitimacy show a significant reduction in the hazard of death [21]. Finally, Bastedo and Bowman [22] demonstrate that the impact of a positive position in a public ranking continues to benefit the organization even on future peer assessments independently of the changes in quality and performance that may occur. The obtainment of a certification is also strategic in this perspective. Sine, David and Mitsuhashi [23], by analyzing the energetic sector, affirm that a certification is not only useful to show some organizational features which are at risk of remaining hidden, but it is fundamental to obtain both resources and trust. Legitimacy is able to modify external opinions about an organization.

It is unlikely that the need to obtain legitimacy affects a single organization in a sector, rather it involves whole sectors, in which similar "best solutions" are adopted. As a consequence organizations working in the same sector tend to show "isomorphism" [10, 3]. Isomorphism suggests that some organizational features have been modified in order to be adapted to the external context [24], while other ones are abandoned or more appreciated by decision-makers [25]. Aldrich [26] claims that, "*the best thing that organizations can do is take into account what other organizations are doing.*" The isomorphism can operate both inducing a structural [5, 27, 28] or a procedural change [29-31]. Moreover, the organizational changes occur in a precise moment. They occur in correspondence to significant happenings such as regulatory events, or resources deployments [32-35].

In this perspective the contribution of Thornton and Ocasio [33] is interesting. It analyzes an outstanding change in the editorial context during the '70s, concerning the publishers' conception of *work*, which progressively passed from a professional working logic to a business one. In the same debate we find Goodrick and Salancik [34] who recognize a correspondence between the use of the Cesarean section during childbirth and the changes in its regulation.

The aspects analyzed up to this point such as the pressures of the environment, the choice of pursuing legitimacy rather than efficiency, and the progressive uniformity of behaviors between organizations, are all traceable features within the healthcare sector. In this context, in fact, the approval of the external environment can be considered the main cause of the organization's birth or mortality [8, 36].

Neoinstitutionalism in Healthcare

Within the healthcare sector changes occur when the existing structures and beliefs are undermined or questioned [37]. It is because changes generate a high degree of uncertainty, especially due to their sources [38] that are frequently represented by external stakeholders (at a central or regional level). They may decide how healthcare organizations need to perform their activities, without considering if those requests are coherent with preexisting structures and practices. On the other hand, even customers' appreciation of the changes, determine uncertainty [39]. Taking into account these difficulties, why should healthcare organizations feel the need to perform those changes? The reason is the need to be legitimized.

Healthcare organizations are extremely sensitive to external legitimacy for three main reasons:

1) Considering the importance of the services provided, massive attention is paid to their conduct, both from the institutions and the customers'. This leads healthcare organizations to adopt the same behavior as the most successful organizations.
2) The role of the "*word of mouth advertisement,*" which positively works if constructive information about a hospital is provided, such as the adoption of innovative technologies, procedures or organizational models.
3) Due to the uncertainty, which characterizes the healthcare context, in terms of paucity of resources and growing expenditures, healthcare organizations are very doubtful about the introduction of new practices and processes, technologies or organizational designs. For that reason they often follow what most successful organizations are doing, in order to appear legitimized and to avoid the risk of adopting innovations that may not be not appreciated by the external context.

Several authors provide evidence in this sense. D'Aunno, Sutton and Price [40] state how mental health and drug abuse treatment organizations are frequently obliged to argue with a deeply institutionalized sector, in which the influence of stakeholders' opinion is significantly strong. The challenge consists in the adoption of hybrid structures which are most suitable to external expectations. The hybrid organizational arrangement is in fact able to concurrently answer to different conflicting needs. The real aim of this choice is the acquisition of resources and legitimacy from the external context [21], thus decreasing the organization's mortality rate. The inverse correlation between the degree of institutional relations and the mortality rate of organizations is documented [41].

Ruef and Scott [36] provide another contribution to the debate They focus on how external approval can be considered critical for the survival of organizations in the American healthcare sector. Authors show that hospital survival rate is positively associated with certifications obtained from prestigious external bodies, such as the Joint Commission on the Accreditation of Healthcare Organizations or the American Medical Association. The challenge of the organization operating in highly institutionalized sectors is, in their opinion, acquiring legitimacy by normative sources.

The examples provided lead to some considerations. Within non-institutionalized contexts, organizations work following the strategies elaborated by managers. They may generate services and products that can be either appreciated or not by customers. As a consequence, customers are a determining factor for an eventual change in the initial strategies. A different approach is adopted within highly institutionalized contexts, such as the healthcare. Here managerial decisions are both driven by the population (customers) needs in terms of age, mortality rate, disease, and by the need to obtain legitimacy from institutional stakeholders. Even in this case customer appreciation may determine strategic changes, but these changes need to be approved by the institutional stakeholders, making the whole process more difficult. Figure 2 provides the circular approach to the strategy formulation adapted to the healthcare context.

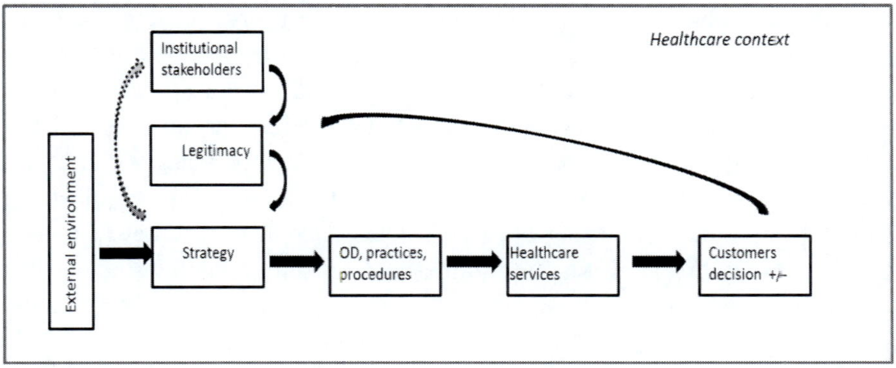

Figure 2. Strategies formulation within healthcare context.

One of the main consequences of this strategy formulation is the progressive similarity between hospital organizational models, together with a substantial similarity between both the practices and the procedures adopted. That kind of homogenization is named isomorphism.

Analyzing Institutional Pressures

Literature recognizes three different pressures, coercive, mimetic and normative [2, 10] through which organizations tend to be similar in the attempt to obtain support and legitimacy from stakeholders. Coercive isomorphism is driven by the decisions made by third party organizations. When the lawyer or other stakeholders establish that an organizational model, a procedure, or a certification is needed in a certain context, organizations usually modify their shape or their conduct to conform to external expectations, thus causing homogenization. The adoption of clinical directorates[2] in the Italian healthcare system provides evidence in this sense. During the '90s several legislative decrees established the need to introduce the clinical directorate model within healthcare organizations [42, 43], and therefore its large diffusion all over the country. A further example of isomorphism is provided by Goodrick and Salancik [34] who analyze the diffusion and the consequent reduction of the Cesarean birth section during childbirth. The spread of that technique was initially caused by an external demand which was then limited by a legislative intervention.

The second pressure known as mimetism is the source of the mimetic isomorphism, whose main actor is uncertainty. When organizations perceive that external conditions are dangerous and uncertain, they decide to follow, or to mime conducts and decisions of those organizations considered the most successful. The new conducts and decisions adopted are not always suitable for the organization that is copying, but they are easy to be identified and safe in a surviving logic. In this vein Haveman [30] shows that organizations decide to reproduce the changes already tested by others, in order to reduce research and innovation costs. The mimesis is not only related to the need to obtain legitimacy, but mostly to the need to avoid the risks concerning both the research and development of a new product or service [44].

Finally, professional isomorphism is driven by managerial knowledge, which is able to modify processes and organizational practices. Generally, the

[2] For more details about the clinical directorate model, please see chapter one.

similarity between knowledge acquired within the same universities, or attending the same meetings, induces managers to introduce analogous solutions and changes within the organizations they lead or in which they operate. Burns and Wholey [27] provide an example of professional isomorphism by examining the adoption of the matrix organizational arrangement, which has been implemented not for technical needs, but to answer to professional pressures. The matrix model was largely adopted by healthcare organizations between the'60s and the'70s thanks to the impact of several scientific journals in which professionals share their successful experiences with the model.

Figure 3 summarizes the typologies and the sources of isomorphism.

Although the decision to mime is based on the need to manage the surviving challenge, managers need to pay attention to the unintended consequences emerging from the decision to implement new organizational features, designs, practices or technologies based on institutional logics. The first consequence is the decrease in the innovation rate of the organization. If we consider that the external context identifies and chooses the best organizational models, practices and processes and it recognizes legitimacy only to the adopting organizations, there is no chance of existence for new models and practices. That condition persists until a legitimate organization decides to introduce a new change. From then on a new model or practice will become the best solution for the organizations that desire to appear legitimized.

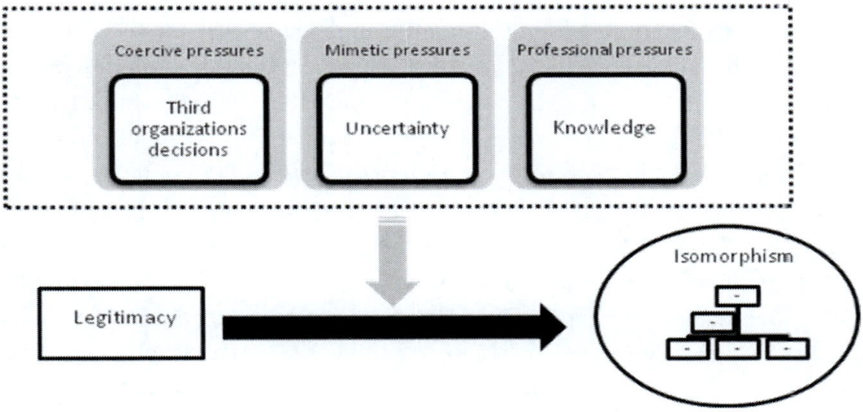

Figure 3. Typologies and sources of isomorphism.

Often the changes introduced are not actually implemented. In several cases it is possible to identify an opportunistic behavior known as decoupling. The decoupling phenomenon corresponds to a false conformity between what organizations seem to do and what they are really doing. A key role in that context is played by the conflicting pressures emerging from the internal/ external stakeholders. The decoupling is responsible for both the adoption and the contextual non-implementation of organizational models and practices within the organizations [2, 45-49, 43]. The following paragraphs are dedicated to a deep analysis of that phenomenon.

INSTITUTIONAL PRESSURES RELIEF: THE *DECOUPLING*, A THEORETICAL APPROACH

What are the reasons driving organizations to adopt new designs and practices without fully implementing them? Is it a need coming from the struggle to obtain legitimacy? Or is it the result of impositions operated without taking into consideration the real organizational needs? The main issue in that sense concerns the inconsistency between the external pressures for change and the internal goals of the organization [49].

Meyer and Rowan [2] showed that organizations "*buffer their formal structures from uncertainties of technical activities, by becoming loosely coupled, building gaps between their formal structures and actual work activities*" in order to avoid conflicts [45]. In this vein organizations declare conformity to an institutional logic coming from a law, a demand, or a general expectation, through giving only a ceremonial and symbolic commitment to certain logic while preserving its core identity and its core technical activities and practices [2, 46, 47]. Following Meyer and Rowan [2], Wesphal and Zajac [48] affirmed that "*by designing a formal structure that adheres to the prescriptions of myths in the institutional environment, an organization demonstrates that it is acting on collectively valued purposes in a proper and adequate manne*r." As we have already analyzed in the previous paragraphs organizations decide to change their structures or their procedures not for a real technical need, but rather to obtain legitimacy from the external context. The *decoupling oriented* conduct induces organizations to realize fictitious changes through the strictly formal adoption of new organizational forms and aims to protect their core identity. Decoupling allows organizations to buffer the internal routines from the external uncertainties, improving flexibility and obtaining legitimacy [49]. From an external point of view organizations end up being aligned with the external expectations, but if we could analyze in detail the internal processes it would be clear that nothing has really changed. Decoupling allows people "*to continue carrying out their work*" [50], developing a substantial protection of the internal processes and dynamics. Figure 4 illustrates how the decoupling practice is performed.

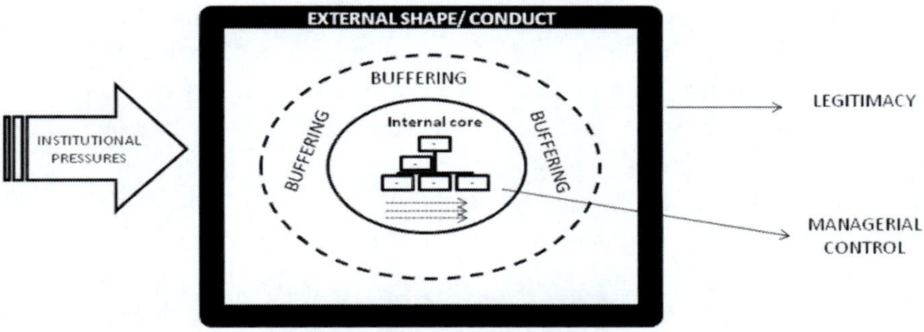

Figure 4. The decoupling practice.

Through decoupling managers are able to maintain their discretion over the allocation of resources [16], which may be impossible in correspondence with a real implementation of the change. Here in fact the resource allocation should be coherent with the implemented innovation. Through this perspective decoupling assumes the shape of an opportunistic managerial conduct. The reason on which decoupling is based seems to be not only the organizational need to preserve its core competencies, but the managerial need to keep resources under control [49]. The representation of this statement is illustrated in the right side of Figure 4.

Thereafter, both the institution's role and the stakeholder's, have to be reconsidered. Their attempt to introduce new practices and structures can contribute to make organizations more efficient, but this is not aligned with managers' willingness to retain their sphere of influence. The problem can be solved by decision makers by both following a more rational approach in projecting changes and drawing differentiated organizational changes, considering the organization's needs.

Although the decoupling phenomenon has been detected in different contexts: schools, public firms, publishers, healthcare organizations seem to be particularly inclined to decouple their behavior, due to managers' and professionals' need to maintain autonomy. In a managerial perspective hospital CEOs need to buffer designs and processes of the organizations that they lead, in order to control the resources. Professionals on the other hand want to buffer the internal practices in order to maintain their autonomy on patients' care. Evidence about the different perspectives on decoupling is provided.

Policy makers should know and deeply understand the decoupling phenomenon because they are considered its source [43]. Through the emanation of laws, advice, and expectations, they choose the organizational arrangements and processes that healthcare organizations have to adopt to obtain legitimacy. To become aware of the consequences of their impositions, they should try to take into consideration the role of healthcare organization managers, together with performing a screening to verify the actual implementation of changes.

Even healthcare managers are aware of the decoupling phenomenon because through it they can maintain their control on resources.

Professionals (physicians, nurses and allied health staff) can face two different kinds of problems related to decoupling depending on their job roles. If they are already working in the organization they will continue to work differently from what is expected, creating a lack of compliance between what managers think that professionals are doing and what they are really doing. If professionals are out of the organization the problem is related to the disappointment that decoupling may generate. For example the vocational choice of a physician can be based on the information that healthcare organizations externally show about either how it is organized, or how procedures and practices are performed. Once a physician has been employed within the organization that he/she chose considering certain information, a different situation may be found, which can lead to the will to leave the organization. Besides that, professionals can also be considered as one of the motivations of the decoupling because often external changes are carried out to preserve their habitual activities.

In several healthcare systems, as for instance the Italian NHS, the hospital is freely chosen by patients. Their choice is based on both previous experiences of relatives and friends, and public opinion regarding its functionality. Therefore, if a structure is well known for having adopted a particular organizational model, or an innovative practice, patients can be more interested in it. Unfortunately, due to decoupling, once in the hospital they may experience a different situation than what they expected, and therefore they can feel strongly disappointed.

The following section provides some evidence about how the decoupling phenomenon occurs within healthcare organizations.

The Diffusion of the *Decoupling* Phenomenon in Healthcare: A Literature Review

The empirical studies on decoupling are extremely interesting to investigate because they allow us to understand how it happens, and therefore its impact on organizational conduct. The present section is dedicated to an analysis of contributions in the literature which show how healthcare organizations are involved in the challenges arising from decoupling.

The evidence was collected through a systematic literature review, by using the key words "decoupling" and "healthcare organizations." The contributions collected are seven. Papers show that the phenomenon affects healthcare organizations at different decision-making levels: strategic, structural, procedural, and at the level of performance, in terms of results achieved.

Adinolfi [51], and Lega et al. [52], analyze the impact of decoupling on strategic choices and strategy communication within healthcare organizations. Mascia and colleagues [43] show how decoupling affects the adoption/implementation of a new organizational arrangement, while Stokken [53], shows how decoupling affects hospital practices. Pettersen and Nyland [54] and Covalesky et al. [55] analyze the influence of decoupling on the performance measurement. Finally, Levay and Waks [56] adopt a new perspective on the issue, showing evidence on the so called *inverse decoupling*. A brief description of the above mentioned papers is provided in order to comprehend this phenomenon.

In her work of 2014, Adinolfi [51] demonstrates that the Total Quality Management (hereafter TQM) practice is composed of a series of assignments and objectives that need to be performed by those organizations that really want to organize their activities by following this strategic approach. A deep analysis of healthcare organizations, however, shows how the TQM is not always entirely implemented, as it should be, but often it is adopted just in some units of the organization, or in a few phases of the process, creating a discrepancy between the theory of TQM and its practical implementation. By adopting the TQM process, healthcare managers need to take into consideration two main stakeholders: physicians and purchasers. Upon closer examination, often physicians do not want many innovations in the healthcare processes, because they want to maintain control of the practices and they do not accept a managerial influence on their activities. On the contrary purchasers prefer the TQM approach to be adopted because it is in line with the managerial orientation to the quality of healthcare processes. Therefore both Italian and Irish healthcare managers decide to decouple structures from practices. In this way the doctor's behavior remains the same, while external stakeholders are assured about the quality of the care provided.

Even Lega and colleagues [52] face the decoupling problem by analyzing how healthcare organizations use and spread their strategic documents. They proved the existence of a multitude of strategic documents which result differentiated in order to meet the stakeholders' expectations without respecting a logical sequence in terms of diffusion and contents. It seems that those documents have only the formal shape of a strategic design process, most of them being produced just to accomplish the external expectations, without orienting the healthcare organizations' activities. The result is that healthcare organizations continue to perform their activities without realizing the requested changes in processes, structures and goals, and on the other side external stakeholders appear satisfied with what organizations formally declare since they are aligned with their expectations.

Moving through an internal perspective Mascia and colleagues' contribution [43], examines the decoupling in the decision-making process of adoption/implementation of a new organizational arrangement. They analyze the way in which healthcare organizations adhere to laws regarding the adoption of the clinical directorate model. Since a real implementation of that model involves the introduction of some clinical governance tools during health service provision (such as: telemedicine, clinical pathways, information systems), they measured the presence of decoupling considering whether or not those tools are adopted. Authors found out that whereas the model was introduced before the law implementation, hospitals adopted all the tools that ensure its effective functionality. On the contrary the hospitals forced by the law in the adoption of that new organizational arrangement achieve it by decoupling the structure from the clinical processes. So the hospital's core activity is protected by the external shape which was changed in order to conform to an external expectation.

A further interesting contribution to the topic is provided by Stokken [53]. He analyzed the decoupling phenomenon in the education of patients. In Norway patient education is one of the four main tasks of healthcare organizations along with treatment, research and health professionals' education. Although healthcare organizations are not completely convinced about the usefulness of that practice, they perform it to obtain legitimacy. In order to adhere to a legal requirement, healthcare organizations adopt different approaches in patient education, trying to show that there is equality between professionals and customers, even knowing that it is not completely true. The author claims that the concept of equality between patients and professionals is a beautiful idea but it is not based on practical evidence.

Further contributions are dedicated to the explanation of the way in which decoupling affects the behavior of healthcare organizations. The perspective of analysis implemented by Pettersen and Nyland [54] and Covalesky and colleagues [55] can be defined as an outcome-oriented perspective. Both papers in fact analyze how decoupling affects the performance analysis within healthcare organizations.

Pettersen and Nyland [54] analyze how the New Public Management (NPM), adopted in Norway since the '90s, introduced a number of changes within healthcare organizations. The NPM attested a specific interest of the State on measuring input and performance to assess efficiency and effectiveness. As a consequence, the hospitals started to use accounting information in order to assess performance. The authors detected a decoupling between administrative and clinical activities within the healthcare context. Because there is no real correspondence between healthcare professional performance and accounting procedures, the measurement has the sole function of maintaining legitimacy. Consequently there is not only an information gap between the State and hospitals, but also an internal information gap between clinical and administrative activities.

The perspective of analysis conducted by Covalesky and colleagues [55] concerns a performance measurement in terms of DRG and case mix accounting system. Authors affirm that both the DRG systems, and the case mix accounting system, exert a significant role in the construction of the external legitimacy of healthcare organizations, instead of being used to improve efficacy and effectiveness.

Again the problem is related to the incoherence between the external and the internal conduct of hospitals. Managers, in order to appear legitimate, can screen patients, or shift resources in ward units, that fulfill a higher external visibility. The performance measurement has the potential of penetrating and altering the hospital's internal processes which are checked in their financial dimension.

Finally Levay and Waks [56] provide different contributions to the decoupling debate by introducing the term of *inverse decoupling*. It is referred to the professional's belief in the usefulness of incorporating a practice in their work. The above cited approach seems to be particularly widespread among those professionals who are oriented in avoiding external influences on their work. They are not interested in promoting their conduct, but they maintain the external perception of their work unchanged, thus protecting the internal conduct of the organization.

By following different perspectives all contributions explain the way in which healthcare organizations try to respond to the conflicting pressures coming from both the external and the internal stakeholders. The analyzed evidence shows that the external context has several expectations in terms of organizational designs, activities, and outcome measurements of the organizations. At the same time professionals want to keep providing healthcare processes in a routine way and they do not want their administrative management to be inspected. Table 1 summarizes the papers discussed above, analyzing them in terms of: perspective of analysis, authors, internal or external source of legitimacy; the object decoupled and finally the subjects that take advantage of the decoupling.

Table 1. Comparative analysis of the contributions on decoupling

Author(s)	Perspective	Year	Legitimacy pressure direction	Object decoupled	Subject(s) protected
Adinolfi [51]	Strategic	2014	External: Stakeholders	TQM practices	Physicians
Lega et al.[52]		2013	External: Policy makers	Strategic documents	Organization
Mascia et al. [43]	Structural	2014	External: State	Clinical directorate model adoption	Physicians, Managers
Stokken [53]	Procedural	2011	External: Policy makers	Patients education	Organization
Pettersen and Nyland [54]	Performance measurement	2006	External: State	Performance measurement	Physicians
Covalesky et al. [55]		1993	External: Policymakers	DRG system, case mix system	Managers
Levay and Waks [56]	Inverse decoupling	2009	Internal	Work practices	Professionals

We learn that, except for Levay and Waks's paper [56], all contributions show a legitimacy pressure coming from the external environment (stakeholders, policymakers and State), and those few subjects, who are physicians and .managers, take advantage of the decoupling practice. The analysis clearly shows that the phenomenon is affected by two conflicting pressures: an external pressure and an internal one, and that the organization's policies aim to protect core activities and habitual behaviors.

The next section explains the consequences of decoupling analyzing the different points of view of managers, professionals, patients and external stakeholders.

THE CHALLENGE OF *DECOUPLING:* PRACTICAL IMPLICATIONS

The previously analyzed contributions offer a chance to think about the consequences of decoupling. External stakeholders can be persuaded of the significant role they exert on healthcare organizations. Through all the contributions examined, except for Levay and Waks, [56], it has been demonstrated that the main sources of decoupling are laws, acts, and expectations coming from the external context, which are formalized by the State or by policy makers and progressively become the same as those of the customers. A significant example of that process is provided and described by Stokken [53] in the patient's education field. In Norway that practice is a governmental requirement which then becomes a patient's demand, the patient being fully involved personally. Due to their important role, external stakeholders must be aware of the relevance of acts, laws and invitations that they introduce and they must supervise their practical implementation by giving precise suggestions and guidelines. As for instance the legal ambiguity that arose with the introduction of the clinical directorate model within the Italian healthcare context [43], generated autonomous solutions adopted by hospitals, in terms of implementation of the model. Through a punctual legislative intervention those hospitals would have had fewer chances of decoupling their structures.

Another example provided by Covalesky and colleagues [55] proved that there is no real control of performance data communication. Consequently new questions arise in terms of a hospital's opportunistic behavior, since organizations skim patients in order to appear more efficient to external observers. The most serious patients together with those affected by a chronic degenerative disease are not accepted in the hospital in order to avoid a negative influence in the performance. The consequences of decoupling are not just related to a false adoption of a model or procedure, but they also lead to an unfair approach towards patients.

While external stakeholders are considered the source of decoupling, managers and physicians can be considered as subjects protected by decoupling. Hospital CEOs or the clinical directors are evaluated according to the level of accomplishment of external requests. For instance in the Italian system, hospital CEOs are evaluated on the basis of their strategies or according to the adoption of the clinical directorate model [42, 43], whereas in the Norwegian system, hospital CEOs are evaluated considering the activities in the patient education field [53]. As a consequence managers introduce organizational innovations following a ceremonial approach, instead of a rational one, since they are not convinced about their usefulness. Furthermore, there is a risk of damaging hospital activities whereas managers fail in recognizing their needs or in checking their affirmations on the new practices or models introduced. Since professionals treasure their autonomy and due to their legal responsibility in patient assistance, authority is a not a welcome pressure [1].

Finally from the patients' point of view decoupling is not an acceptable practice. As we already stated, a patient's choice is often related to both the external shape of healthcare organizations and the external information about their practices and technologies. In both cases a customer's opinion about the hospital will be different from what they expected. People see "A" but hospital performs "B," and customers give their opinion about what they have experienced: "B" and not "A." But if A is not similar to B as frequently happens, external observers can be confused about the actual performances of the hospital leading them to look elsewhere for more transparency.

CONCLUSION

This chapter focused on the challenges to which organizations that want to increase success in their sector are subjected to. Although it is a common problem, the role of the external context is particularly important within the healthcare sector. The external stakeholders (State, Policy makers, Patients) can determine the survival of healthcare organizations by recognizing their legitimacy. As a consequence healthcare organizations are interested in obtaining and maintaining the right level of legitimacy by performing activities or adopting models that fulfill external expectations. Furthermore, they are often led to adopt strategic approaches which are not really necessary to run the organizations. These "opportunistic behaviors" often represent a source of important consequences. First and foremost, healthcare organizations tend to be very similar to each other. In the attempt to face uncertainty, organizations comply with law prescriptions, or they copy what most successful organizations do, or finally they put their trust in professional advice. As a consequence organizational arrangements or practices are just formally adopted, without actually being implemented. This creates a discrepancy between the external and the internal shape of the organizations. A second consequence is related to professional behavior. Being extremely possessive of their internal activities, professionals try to protect them from inconsistent external pressures, by operating the decoupling. It allows people to keep performing their work without interferences. However, it can generate controversial opinions about hospital performance, mainly because of the distance between what they declare and what they actually do. Policy makers and manager awareness of the decoupling phenomenon consequences plays an important role in preventing its development.

REFERENCES

[1] Cicchetti, Americo. 2004. *La Progettazione Organizzativa*. Franco Angeli Sanità. (in Italian).

[2] Meyer, John W., and Brian Rowan. 1977. "Institutionalize organizations: formal structure as myth and ceremony." *American journal of sociology,* 83: 340-363.

[3] Powell, Walter W., and Paul J. Di Maggio. 1991. *The new institutionalism in organizational analysis*, IL: University of Chicago Press, Chicago.

[4] Tolbert, Pamela. S., and Lynne G Zucker. 1983." Institutional Sources of Change in Formal Structure of Organization: the Diffusion of Civil Service Reform, 1880-1935." *Administrative Science Quarterly,* 28: 22-39.

[5] Fligstein, Neil. 1985. "The spread of multidivisional form among large firms: 1919-1979." *American Sociological Review,* 50 (3): 377-391.

[6] Thompson, James D. 1967. *Organizations in Action. McGraw Hill,* New York.

[7] Blau Peter M., and Richard Schoenherr. 1971. *The structure of organizations*. New York: Basic Books.

[8] Scott, Richard W., Martin Ruef., Peter J. Mendel and Carol A. Caronna. 2000. *Institutional Change and Healthcare Organizations. From Professional Dominance to Managed Care*. The University of Chicago Press: London.

[9] Heugens, Pursey P.M.A.R., and Michael W. Lander. 2009. "Structure! Agency! (And Other Quarrels): Meta-Analyzing Institutional Theories of Organization." *Academy of Management Journal*, 52(1), 61-85.

[10] Powell, Walter W., and Paul J. Di Maggio. 1983. "The iron cage revisited: institutional isomorphism and collective rationality." *American sociological review,* 48: 147-160.

[11] Selznick, Philip. 1957. *Leadership in Administration*. Harper & Row: New York.

[12] Scott, Richard W. 1992. *Organizations: Rational, Natural and Open Systems*. Englewood Cliffs, N.J. Prentice-Hall.

[13] Fiss, Peer.C., and Edward J., Zajac. 2006. "The Symbolic Management of Strategic Change: Sensegiving Via Framing and Decoupling." *Academy of Management Journal,* 46: 1173-1193.

[14] Smirich, Linda. 1983. "Organizations as Shared Meanings." In *Organizational symbolism*, edited by Louis R. Pondy, Peter J. Frost, Gareth. Morgan, & Thomas Dandridge: 55-65. Greenwich, CT: JAI.

[15] Oliver, Christine, 1991. "Strategic responses to institutional processes." *Academy of management review,* vol. 16, n.1; 145-179.

[16] Orrù, Marco, Nicole W. Biggart, and Gary G. Hamilton. 1991. "Organizational isomorphism in East Asia," in *The new institutionalism in organizational analysis*, edited by Powell Walter W., and Paul J. Di Maggio.

[17] Suchman, Mark C., 1995. "Managing legitimacy: strategic and institutional approaches." *Academy of management review.* 20 (3), 571-610.

[18] Zucker, Lynne G. 1987. "Institutional Theories of Organization," *Annual Review of Sociology,* 13: 443-464.

[19] Scott, Richard W., and John W. Meyer. 1983. *Organizational environments: ritual and rationality.* CA Sage, Beverly Hills.

[20] Deephouse, David L., 1996. "Does isomorphism legitimate?" *The Academy of Management Journal,* 39 (4): 1024-1039.

[21] Singh, Jitendra. V., David J. Tucker, and Robert J. House. 1986. "Organizational legitimacy and the liability of newness." *Administrative Science Quarterly,* 31, 171-193.

[22] Bastedo, Michael N., and Nicholas A. Bowman. 2010." U.S. News & World report college rankings: modeling institutional effect on organizational reputation." *American Journal Of Education,* 116: 163-181.

[23] Sine, Wesley D., Robert J. David and Hitoshi Mitsuhashi. 2007. "From plan to plant: effect of certification on operational start-up in the emergent independent power sector." *Organization Science*, 18 (4): 578-594.

[24] Hawley, Amos. 1968. "Human ecology." In *International encyclopedia of the social sciences*, edited by David L Sills, Macmillan, New York.

[25] Hannan, Michael T., and John Freeman. 1977. "The Population Ecology of the Organizations." *Academy Journal of Sociology*, n.83.

[26] Aldrich, Howard E. 1979. *Organizations and Environments*. Englewood Cliff, N.J, Prentice hall.

[27] Burns, Lawton R., and Douglas R. Wholey. "Adoption and abandonment of matrix management programs: effects of organizational characteristics and inter organizational networks." *The Academy of Management Journal,* 36 (1): 106-138.

[28] Sine, Wesley D., Robert J. David. 2003. "Environmental jolts, institutional change, and the creation of entrepreneurial opportunity in the US electric power industry." *Research Policy,* 32: 185-207.

[29] Rao, Hayagreeva, Henrich R., Greve, and Gerald F. Davis. 2001. "Fool's Gold: social proof in the initiation and abandonment of coverage by Wall Street analysts." *Administrative Science Quarterly*, 46 (3): 502-526.

[30] Haveman, Heather A. 1993. "Follow the leader: mimetic isomorphism and entry into new markets." *Administrative Science Quarterly*, 38 (4): 593-627.

[31] Gooderham, Paul N., Odd Nordhaug, and Kristen Ringdal. 1999. "Institutional and rational determinants of organizational practices: human resource management in European firms." *Administrative Science Quarterly,* 44: 507-531.

[32] Ruef, Martin. 2000. "The emergence of organizational forms: a community ecological approach." *The American Journal of Sociology,* 106 (3): 658-714.

[33] Thornton, Patricia H., and William Ocasio. 1999. "Institutional logics and the historical contingency of power in organizations: executive succession in the higher education publishing industry, 1958-1990." *The American Journal of Sociology,* 105 (3): 801-843.

[34] Goodrick, Elizabeth and Gerald R. Salancik. 1996. "Organizational discretion in responding to institutional practices: hospitals and cesarean births." *Administrative Science Quarterly,* 41: 1-28.

[35] Scott, Richard W. and John Meyer. 1991. "The Organization of Societal Sectors: Proposition and Early Evidence." In *The new institutionalism in organizational analysis*, edited by Powell Walter W., and Paul J. Di Maggio. University of Chicago Press.

[36] Ruef, Martin and Richard Scott. 1998. "A multidimensional model of organizational legitimacy: hospital survival in changing institutional environments." *Administrative Science Quarterly*, 43(4): 877-904.

[37] Greenwood, Royston and Christopher R. Hinings. 1996. "Understanding radical organizational change: bringing together the old and the new institutionalism." *Academy of management review*, 21 (4): 1022-1054.

[38] Hinings, Christopher R., Ann Casebeer, Trish Reay, Karen Golden-Biddle, Amy Pablo, and Royston Greenwood. 2003. "Regionalizing healthcare in Alberta: legislated change, uncertainty and loose coupling." *British Journal of Management*, 14: S15-S30.

[39] Arndt, Markus and Barbara Bigelow. 2000. "Presenting structural innovation in an institutional environment: Hospitals' use of impression management." *Administrative Science Quarterly,* 45: 494-522.

[40] D'Aunno, Thomas, Robert I. Sutton, and Richard H. Price. 1991. "Isomorphism and external support in conflicting institutional environments: a study of drug abuse treatment units." *Academy of Management Journal,* 34 (3): 636-661.

[41] Baum, Joel A.C., and Oliver C., 1991. "Institutional linkages and organizational mortality." *Administrative Science Quarterly,* 36: 187-218.

[42] Lega, Federico. 2008. "The rise and fall(acy) of clinical directorates in Italy." *Health Policy* 85: 252-262.

[43] Mascia, Daniele, Federica Morandi, and Americo Cicchetti. 2014. "Looking good or doing better? Patterns of Decoupling in the implementation of Clinical Directorates." *Health Care Management Review,* 39(2): 111-123.

[44] Haunschild, Pamela R. 1993. "Interorganizational imitation: the impact of interlocks on corporate acquisition activity." *Administrative Science Quarterly,* 38 (4): 564-592.

[45] Hallett, Tim and Marc J. Ventresca, 2006. "How institutions form: loose coupling as mechanism in Gouldner's patterns of industrial bureaucracy." *American Behavioral Scientist*, 49, 908-924.

[46] Sauder, Michael and Wendy N. Espeland. 2009. "The discipline of rankings: tight coupling and organizational change." *American Sociological Review,* 74: 63-82.

[47] Pache, Anne Claire and Filipe Santos. 2010. "When worlds collide: the internal dynamics of organizational responses to conflicting institutional demands." *Academy of Management Review*, 35 (3): 455–476.

[48] Westphal, J.D., Edward J. Zajac. 1998. "The symbolic management of stockholders: corporate governance reforms and shareholders reactions." *Administrative Science Quarterly*, 3 (1): 127-153.

[49] Westphal, J.D., Edward J. Zajac. 2001. "Decoupling policy from practice: the case of stock repurchase programs." *Administrative Science Quarterly,* 46 (2): 202-228.

[50] Cohen, Mark A., and James March, 1974. *Leadership and ambiguity*. Harward University Press, Boston MA.

[51] Adinolfi, Paola. 2003. "Total quality management in public health care: a study of Italian and Irish hospital." *Total Quality Management*, 14 (2): 141-150.

[52] Lega, Federico, Francesco Longo, and Andrea Rotolo. 2013. "Decoupling the use and meaning of strategic plans in public healthcare." *BMC Health Services Research,* 13:5

[53] Stokken, Roar. 2011. "(Un)organizing equal collaboration between users and professionals: on management of patient education in Norway." *Health Expectations,* 16: 32-42.

[54] Pettersen, Inger J., and Kari Nyland. 2006. "Management and control of public hospitals- the use of performance management in Norwegian hospitals. A case study." *International Journal of Health Planning and Management,* 21: 133-149.

[55] Covaleski, Mark A., Mark W. Dirsmith, and Jeffrey E. Michelman. 1993. "An institutional theory perspective on the DRG framework, case mix accounting systems and health- care organizations." *Accounting Organizations and Society,* 18 (1): 65-80.

[56] Levay, Charlotta and Caroline Waks. 2009." Professions and the pursuit of transparency in healthcare: two cases of soft autonomy." *Organization Studies,* 30(05): 509-527.

Chapter 3

MANAGING UNCERTAINTY: THE QUALITY CERTIFICATION ADOPTION BETWEEN MANAGERIAL FASHIONS AND SOCIAL CONTAGION

ABSTRACT

The uncertainty in the healthcare sector determines managerial decisions that are driven by institutional, ceremonial or mimetic motivations. The need to face the variability of the results of healthcare services makes the introduction of standardization necessary. Standardization has been widely recognized as one of the best solutions to maintain variability within physiological limits. Notably the ISO 9001 quality certification seems to be the most diffused in almost all sectors. A country based analysis was performed in order to analyze empirically how, when, and why the process of adoption of the ISO 9001 quality certification occurs. Data about the achievement of quality certifications by Italian healthcare organizations were collected, and then analyzed, following different theoretical perspectives. Due to the differences in terms of motivations and actors involved in the process of diffusion, we followed various theoretical approaches to interpret the phenomenon. We mainly focused on the role of the institutional pressures, the dynamics emerging from the social contagion among organizations and the diffusion of managerial fads and fashions. Finally, some residual adoptions have been recognized as to be based just on organizational needs. Results show very complex dynamics of adoption, and they have been discussed in order to assess the managerial and the policy making implications.

Keywords: quality certifications, social contagion, managerial fads and fashions

INTRODUCTION

The healthcare sector, as we have analyzed in the previous chapters, is characterized by a high level of uncertainty, both in a managerial and in a more operative perspective. From a managerial point of view hospital CEOs are often subject to different pressures emerging from both external and internal stakeholders. They are pressured in the process of choosing which strategic decisions are necessary to adopt, in order to achieve a good level of success. Hospital CEOs want to fulfill the external requests in order to appear legitimate, but contextually they do not want the core organizational activities to be subject to radical changes. It occurs because professionals are not prone to accept modifications and interferences in their daily activities [1]. Although managers try to preserve professionals from the uncertain consequences of changes, physicians and nurses are inevitably exposed to it. The choice of the proper way to provide assistance to patients, together with the decisions concerning the best technologies or drugs to use, represents a trial that healthcare professionals have to face daily. Uncertainty is also related to the increasing role of a patient's awareness of new therapies and technologies, together with being fully aware of their rights. As demonstrated in the institutional theory, in case of uncertainty organizations imitate what other organizations are doing. Following this statement, organizations can save resources and time, avoiding the adoption of unknown solutions, and consequent uncertain results. Uncertainty can be considered as a multidimensional feature that can affect all fields of the healthcare service delivery. It can be noticed in several circumstances: in the process of obtaining human and economic resources; with respect to patients' needs; when considering the results of health procedures and practices.

This chapter is focused on the analysis of the last listed kind of uncertainty, together with healthcare organizational strategies to face it.

The literature shows that one of the best ways to reduce the uncertainty of healthcare processes is the use of standardization. The implementation of a standard is able to reduce the mistakes deriving from healthcare processes, by maintaining the level of variability within physiological limits. The standardization can be implemented in several stages of the healthcare service provision, through the use of a series of tools and by following certain methods. The quality certification is one of the most known standardization tools. Although there is a shared confidence about the usefulness of the quality certification system, its use is driven by extremely different logic. A large quantity of studies demonstrated that the quality certification is just a symbolic ceremony achieved by organizations in order to appear legitimate to the external observers [2-4]. Besides that, it is possible to recognize that its use is due to various reasons. As shown in the next paragraphs, healthcare managers may decide to adopt quality certifications in order to follow managerial fads and fashions. Moreover, the diffusion of quality certifications can be based on the social contagion among organizations, but can also be imposed by legal constraints. Finally, we have considered the circumstances under which the decision to adopt a quality certification is based just on organizational determinants, without taking into consideration institutional or mimetic forces. Chapter three is organized as follows: the first section is focused on the analysis of the role of standardization within healthcare organizations, while the second paragraph is dedicated to the analysis of one of the most recognized and used standardization tools: the ISO 9001 quality certification. Then the focus is posed on the role that quality certifications exert within the Italian NHS. The third section is dedicated to a theoretical interpretation of the diffusion of the quality certifications, by analyzing the concepts of managerial fashion, social contagion and coercive isomorphism. The explanation of the above listed concepts will be helpful for the comprehension of the empirical evidence provided through research. The fourth and fifth sections are dedicated to the analysis of the quality certification adoption by Italian healthcare organizations.

THE ROLE OF STANDARDIZATION IN HEALTHCARE

The standardization process is widely considered one of the best practices to improve the quality of the health service provision. As stated by Brunsson and Jacobson [5] "*standard's primary objective is to encourage actors to behave in a similar fashion, producing uniformity across time and space.*"

Standards are explicit statements of expected quality in the performance of healthcare activities. They can be realized in a multiplicity of different ways. For example, standards can be developed as procedures, clinical practice guidelines, treatment protocols, critical paths, standard operating procedures, or statements about the expected healthcare outcomes. The role of standardization is to inform internal and external stakeholders about the level of quality of the services provided. It is because by adopting standards the degree of certainty about the quality of the final product or services increases. The introduction of standardization within organizations determines the increasing of the level of formalization of the processes [6], which is not free from some consequences. As demonstrated by Daft [6] the higher the degree of formalization, the higher the rigidity of the organizational processes. On the contrary, the variability of individual behaviors turns out to be lower.

Standardization can be analyzed by following several points of view. From an organizational point of view standardization can be considered an example of *horizontal coordination mechanism* [7], which has an impact ex ante, during or ex post services delivery. Cicchetti [7] affirms that, within healthcare organizations, professionals can be coordinated ex ante, through the *standardization of cultural norms*. Since professionals attended the same universities or are members of the same professional associations, standardization derives from the homogeneity of competencies developed during their training paths, and throughout their professional career. Standardization can operate *during the process* of healthcare service delivery, by adopting critical pathways and procedures, which are able to uniform professional behavior. Finally, the *standardization ex post* detects the outcomes of health care services delivering, in order to compare the performances of different hospitals or departments.

How and why standardization is useful in the healthcare service provision? From an operative point of view, standardization can be considered a way to reduce supply costs for hospitals, but also a method to improve health outcomes. Standardization leads to a consensus on the best way to provide high quality care, thanks to quality monitoring. Moreover, it can reduce the variability between health care providers. Finally, standardization increases the accomplishment of customer/patient expectations, maximizing the use of resources.

Although the benefits related to the application of standards are documented, some clinical users are still resistant to it for two main reasons: the professional's natural resistance to change, and the low confidence on its positive impact on the patient's outcomes. The usefulness of standardization is perceived differently by healthcare managers and clinicians. Healthcare managers are prone to adopt standardization for several reasons: controlling the healthcare outcomes variability of the care provided, avoiding complaints and legal consequences and appearing legitimate to external stakeholders.

Clinicians on the other hand are suspicious of standardization, they not being inclined to give up their autonomy during healthcare delivery [7]. This resistance however can be surpassed by actively involving them during standard development. According to Botzem and Dobusch [8] the link between the managerial point of view and the clinician's is that both recognize the connection between standardization and legitimacy. There are two main phases of legitimacy: input and output. *Input legitimacy* arises from the involvement of skilled individuals, or experts, in the process of standard development, that are able to increase the clinician's trust in the use of the new standard [9-11], whereas *Output legitimacy* is related to the effectiveness and to the quality of the coordination deriving from the standards application. When clinicians appreciate the usefulness of the new standard, the output legitimacy is created. It creates a circle where the high adoption of standardization contributes to a positive output legitimacy, which in turn drives to further adoptions of new standards.

Once the decision on the standardization adoption is made, managers and professionals need to be involved in its development.

Box 1. Main Steps of the Standardization Process

Step 1: The first step of the standardization process aims to define and to agree upon the development tasks. The identification of the area or topic for which standards are developed plays a significant role. Moreover, it is necessary to identify the aim of the standard (objective) and the areas on which the standard may have an important impact. In addition, it is oriented to the definition of the institutional level for which the standards were developed (e.g., national, regional, organizational). Finally, step 1 clarifies the consensus process considering both the topic selection and the approval process of the standards.

Step 2: The second step is finalized to the identification of the outset of the process, including the stakeholders (represented by those people who have an interest in the successful development of the standards). Stakeholders' expectations should be incorporated in the consensus and approval process of standards development, thereby facilitating their acceptance. In this step, national or international experts are invited to take part in the working group. Moreover, depending on the aim of the task, additional technical experts may be required, as the work advances and new issues arise.

Step 3. The third step is aimed at gathering information about the topic under review, and the resources useful for the standard development. In this step the use of a flowchart is extremely helpful to see which points need to be explored during the standard development. In particular it can be useful to answer significant questions for instance on the existence of laws and regulations related to the topic object of the standard. Moreover it is useful to think about what current practices related to the topic should be considered. Besides that, it is important to clarify if there is previous evidence about the standard topic and information that can be accessed by the work group. The last point of that step is the availability of a significant technology to be used for the development of the standard, together with a supply of the resources needed for the research activity.

Step 4. Draft standards. This step is meant to define the most appropriate solution to draft the standard. First of all the working group has to choose the structure and the format of the standards, depending on the purpose. After choosing the format it is necessary to develop the indicators that will be used to compare the performance to the standards and also to carry out an internal evaluation of the quality of the standard.

Step 5. The fifth step is testing the standard. If the test of the standard has not been realized yet, the working group has to plan it. The aim of the test is to allow the presentation of the standard. Moreover it improves the standard quality and the consensus-building process together with increasing credibility. Whenever it needs revisions it can be improved and then the revised standard can be tested again, until revisions are no longer needed and standards are submitted for approval.

Step 6. The last step is the communication of the standard. Although the standards-setting process ends with the approval of the standards, the impact of well-developed standards depends on how people are actually using them. The standard communication and implementation strategies are crucial to improve the performance and the quality of the process. A well thought-out communication plan is needed to identify how the information will be provided to the right people thereby allowing an appropriate performance of the tasks related to the standards.

Source: Author's elaboration of [12].

As confirmed by Slager and colleagues [10] three dimensions determine the capacity of a standard to regulate the activities: the standard design, its legitimacy, and the standard monitoring. The first phase coincides with the definition of the rules and practices. Legitimacy is related to the involvement of experts in the process, while monitoring concerns the organizational conduct check.

Considering that framework, specialized literature [12] demonstrates that the development of a standard may vary considering the organizational circumstances, the resource availability, or the complexity of the topic to standardize. Box 1 provides the main operative steps related to the development of a standardization process [12].

By following the steps presented in box 1 the standard can significantly improve the final output (a product or a service) of an organization.

As shown by experts standards are useful when they are characterized by certain features: *Pragmatism*; *Trustworthiness*; *Validity*; *Clarity*; *Measurability*. *Pragmatism*: concerns the ability to create the standard by using the existing resources. It is not useful, and in fact even dangerous, to introduce unsustainable standards. It can reduce the motivation of both managers and employees, and damage the stability of the organization. *Trustworthiness* is related to the reproducibility of the standard all around the world, by achieving the same result. *Validity* concerns the scientific based nature of the standard. As we have already seen it is fundamental to obtain internal and external legitimacy. *Clarity*. It is important that the standard be perceived without distortion or misinterpretation. Language plays a crucial role in the spread of the standard among different professional profiles, but also among different countries. *Measurability*: The measurement of the outcomes reached by the standard's application is essential to prove its usefulness.

Among the existing standards, the quality certification is one of the most well-known all over the world. It progressively emerged as a strategic organizational practice able to help organizations to establish and rationalize the production processes [13]. The following section examines the most influential and pervasive quality practice: ISO 9001 certification [13].

CONTEXTUAL BACKGROUND: THE ISO 9001 QUALITY CERTIFICATION

In 1946 delegates from 25 Countries met at the Institute of Civil Engineers in London and decided to create a new international organization to facilitate the international coordination and unification of industrial standards. In February 1947 a new organization which was called ISO, officially started its first operations. Since then a lot of international standards have been published, covering almost all the aspects of technology and manufacturing. Nowadays, ISO is composed of members from 165 countries and 3.368 technical bodies that work daily for standards development. The first ISO standard was published in 1951 and it was updated afterwards. Since its creation ISO has published monthly information about its technical Committees, the standards available and the administrative changes that have occurred in the organization. In 1955, ISO members gathered in Stockholm for the third General Assembly. At the beginning of 1955 the members were 35 and the standards were 68. In the 1960s the developing countries were included in the International Standardization work. A year after a Committee was established for them and a Correspondent membership was introduced afterwards, thereby developing countries started to be informed about the International Standardization work. As the ISO Central Secretary affirmed in 1969, International Standardization is the end of 'technical nationalism.' In 1971, ISO created its first two technical Committees in the environmental field: Air quality and Water quality. Nowadays those Committees have been joined by other groups of environmental experts and they are facing several issues such as soil quality, environmental management and renewable energy. In 1987, the ISO 9000 family of quality management standards was published and it became one of the most well-known standards.

At the beginning of 2012, ISO had 163 members and a total of over 19,000 standards. Today, ISO International Standard covers almost all aspects of technology and business. The last survey on the certification adoption worldwide, dated 2013, shows a general increase in its use. In particular China is in first place among the adopters, followed by Italy, Germany and Japan. The last place is occupied by Brazil [15]. ISO 9001 is one of the most well-known available standards in the world. It has been implemented by more than one million organizations in more than 175 countries. ISO 9001 helps organizations to implement quality management. In fact more than 50 percent of quality issues affect organizations transversally. They are mainly associated with documents control, design control, purchasing consistency, inspection and testing of the final products, and finally process control [15, 17]. It is because quality affects the features of a product (or service) which are required by the customer. Quality management is what organizations need to satisfy both customer quality requirements and quality regulations. Moreover, it means that the organization has to enhance customer satisfaction through a continuous improvement of its performance. ISO 9001 can be applied to organizations of any size, whatever their product or service may be, and in any sector i.e., business enterprises, public administration, or government departments. The certification is not related to the organization's mission, but to the organization's desire to manage processes, or activities with the aim of improving customer satisfaction regarding quality requirements. According to Sandholtz [2], standards can be defined as "mechanism of social order." The use of standards makes it clear who is responsible for doing what, when, how, why and where within organizations. Standards help to "organize organizations," giving legitimacy to adopters [2, 18]. Moreover, in the presence of a standardization of the work activities, employees seem to be happier because of the level of safety and health in their work context [18].

ISO 9001 concerns not the final product or service provided by organizations, but rather the way the organization runs its work. ISO 9001 prescribes how organizations must manage the processes which affect the quality of products and services. Certification demands that production processes be reviewed and documented in accordance with the requirements specified by ISO. The organization prepares the documentation and a *third part registrar* evaluates it. If documents show conformity to the standard, the organization will receive the ISO 9001 certification [13].

The reasons leading to the adoption of a quality certification are multiple. First of all, it can be adopted for business reasons, for instance, whenever there is a mandatory clause in a contract, a market need, or a customer request. Moreover, the certification can be adopted as part of a risk management program, or whenever it motivates staff by setting a clear goal. Motwani [17] identifies worldwide recognition, as one of the benefits of quality certification adoption. A further advantage of the adoption concerns the use of "certification" labels in marketing. Finally, from an internal point of view certification allows an organization to reach a high level of efficiency and as a consequence a decrease in customer complaints [20].

Following this perspective, it is interesting to carry out a country focused analysis on the adoption of the ISO 9001 standard and on the reasons which led to its introduction within healthcare organizations.

Quality Certification in Italy: Determinants of Adoption

During the last decades the Italian NHS has been characterized by radical changes. In order to satisfy patient and stakeholder expectations, attention has focused on few significant issues, for instance, resource availability, organizational design and management efficiency. Through an accurate control of those issues healthcare managers have tried to ensure a continuous improvement of the healthcare processes.

During the '90s, the corporatization process radically affected the Italian NHS, changing hospital governance. A legislative intervention stressed the importance of the "high quality of care." Following its introduction, healthcare managers had to comply with a series of requirements to obtain entrepreneurial autonomy from the central government. For that reason, some external quality certification systems have been introduced in the Italian NHS, for instance the ISO 9001, the institutional accreditation, the JCAHO accreditation system, the European foundation for quality management (EFQM).

The Legislative Decree 502/92 and the Legislative Decree 517/93 stated the necessity to guarantee the quality of healthcare services for all citizens, independently of their geographical location or their economic conditions. Furthermore, legislative decrees stressed the importance of introducing a surveillance system in every Italian region, together with the use of new tools to check the quality of healthcare services. In 1994, a further legislative intervention introduced the surveillance of healthcare processes, in terms of efficacy and effectiveness of the services, focusing on patients' opinions.

Since then, several Italian regions indicated the ISO 9001 standard as the referring principle for the accreditation certificate of hospitals (in the Italian context the accreditation certificate is the compulsory recognition to pursue any healthcare activity). The main innovation introduced by ISO 9001 certification is a new conception of quality management, which focuses on the processes. The ISO 9001 certification allows the organization to update and to improve quality management systems, through the integration between law prescriptions and scientific guidelines.

The process of quality certification affects several organizational features such as:

- Managerial responsibility, in terms of policy and planning decisions;
- Human resource management and the management of infrastructures;
- The realization of products/services delivery (research and development, supply, production);
- The application of an internal auditing system to analyze and improve service delivery.

Generally quality certifications cannot be implemented without managerial commitment. When managers really trust in the quality certification, they are able to communicate its importance to the staff. It happens through appropriate reviews of the pre-existing systems, and the provision of the necessary resources to support its development. Therefore, managers may focus not only on the necessity of receiving the "quality certificate," but also on the development of the necessary tools and managerial approaches to drive the organization through a continuous improvement perspective. Finally, a strong and continuous support of top management plays an important role in the quality certification adoption, particularly when considering the inevitable deficiencies of the system.

In order to obtain a good level of performance specific dimensions associated with the concept of quality need to be taken into consideration.

- **Structure**: environment, equipment, economic resources, human resources and organization of work;
- **Processes**: follow up and patient procedures;
- **Outcomes**: in terms of improvement of patient conditions;
- **Patient's perception** of overall healthcare services provided.

The achievement of quality certifications can help healthcare managers to reach good reliability in terms of objectives and responsibilities for the quality of care. The quality certification allows healthcare managers to improve the external image of their organization, and thereby to promote their activities even following external ranking criteria [19, 10].

There are different degrees of formalization that Italian regions used to formulate the laws which compel hospitals to introduce quality certifications.

For instance, some regions do not provide a clear reference to the ISO 9001 standards introduction, while others make a brief reference to the need to follow "quality standards." Finally, a third group of regions clearly refer to ISO 9001 standards, considering its obtainment a mandatory requirement to provide care on behalf of the Italian NHS.

Table 1 provides a comparative analysis of the Italian regional health plans. The column named "level of formalization" shows the degree of formalization of the regional prescriptions on the adoption of the quality certification standards. The high level is associated with a clear reference to the application of the ISO 9001 quality certification (or a more complex quality certification: as the JCAHO); the medium level is referred to the mention of the need to consider certain quality principles for the health service provision, without a clear reference to the specific ISO quality certification. Finally, the low level concerns those regions in which quality certification is not mentioned in the discipline of health services delivery.

Table 1. Comparative analysis of the Italian regional health plans

Region	**Statement**	**Level of formalization**
Piedmont	The regional quality manual for the accreditation of the healthcare organizations concerns the "quality requirements" that the hospitals need to assure during healthcare service providing.	Medium
Valle d'Aosta	No formalized reference to quality certification standards.	Low
Lombardy	The Regional Government promotes the adoption of international standards for excellence accreditation, based on the model defined by the "Joint Commission International" (JCI).	High
Liguria	The accreditation system has been defined by the Regional Government and it is based on general criteria defined by ISO 2000 (UNI EN ISO 9001: 2000, UNI EN ISO 9004: 2000).	Medium
Autonomous province of Trento	No formalized reference to quality certification standards.	Low

Region	Statement	Level of formalization
Autonomous province of Bolzano	No formalized reference to quality certification standards.	Low
Veneto	No formalized reference to quality certification standards.	Low
Friuli Venezia Giulia	Among the requirements there is the identification of a quality manager, responsible of enabling programs finalized to the improvement of the quality of cares. Healthcare organizations are obliged to plan a high quality level achievement and they have to identify: specific objectives, responsibilities, resources, timing, and performance indicators.	Medium
Emilia Romagna	The regional health plan of 1999-2001 considers the quality and the appropriateness of cares and the compliance with patients' expectations as fundamental elements for the accreditation of the structures. New additional requirements have to be developed basing on ISO 9001 quality certification.	High
Tuscany	No formalized reference to quality certification standards.	Low
Umbria	The institutional model of accreditation expects the active participation of professionals in the health service provision. Moreover it has been attributed an important role to the Cermet Certification body, which was inspired by the ISO 9001 norms.	High
Marche	The regional health plan states the necessity to introduce a quality network finalized to check all the aspects of the quality of cares.	Medium

Table 1. (Continued)

Region	Statement	Level of formalization
Abruzzo	No formalized reference to quality certification standards.	Low
Molise	No formalized reference to quality certification standards.	Low
Latium	No formalized reference to quality certification standards.	Low
Campania	No formalized reference to quality certification standards.	Low
Basilicata	No formalized reference to quality certification standards.	Low
Puglia	No formalized reference to quality certification standards.	Low
Calabria	The regional legislation requires the hospitals the adoption of a quality system certificate according to the standard UNI EN ISO 9000, in order to be considered "centers of excellence."	High
Sicily	No formalized reference to quality certification standards.	Low
Sardinia	No formalized reference to quality certification standards.	Low

The comparative analysis of the regional plans indicates that just 4 of the 21 Italian regions (19 regions and 2 autonomous areas) use a "high degree of formalization" in the discipline of quality. More specifically, Emilia Romagna, Umbria and Calabria refer to the ISO 9001, while in Lombardy the regional law prescribes the achievement of accreditation at the Joint Commission of International Certification. The medium degree of formalization is traceable within four regions. Finally, in most regions, although there is a general statement about the quality, efficacy and appropriateness of care, there is no formal indication on quality standards, and the need to achieve a certification.

Due to the absence of a common rule [21-22], Italian regions have made different decisions about the adoption of the quality certification. For instance, when the law is highly compulsory managers follow coercion, on the contrary when it is medium or low formalized they may follow their ideas, willingness and knowledge.

The next section faces the above cited circumstances, by analyzing the various theoretical lenses which can explain the phenomenon of quality certification adoption within the Italian healthcare context.

THEORETICAL BACKGROUND

The theoretical background of this chapter follows four different perspectives, which can be alternatively used to explain the adoption of the quality certification by Italian healthcare organizations. Those perspectives have been identified by analyzing the sources which determine the decision to achieve a quality certification. For instance, the adoption can be driven by a law prescription, a social contagion between organizations and by managerial fads and fashions diffusion. Finally, the adoption of the certification can be driven by "rational" behaviors of managers, derived from the need to standardize healthcare processes. The four theoretical approaches can be formulated as follows:

- Institutional theory and the analysis of the role and function of the coercive pressures exerted by regional law prescriptions [23-25, 18]. Following this perspective, the adoption is considered an attempt to adhere to a legal requirement. Many authors have studied the impact of the institutional environment on the decision to voluntarily adopt a certification and have analyzed the role of the mimetic, coercive and normative pressures exerted on firms by the marketplace [26]. Here we consider the legal constraints imposed by regional health plans.
- The Social contagion dynamic. Following this perspective the introduction of quality certification can be considered an innovation, whose diffusion can be explained by the year of adoption and the geographical location of the adopters [27-30 (among others)].
- Fads and fashions. Through this perspective the quality certification adoption is considered a managerial fashion that managers share by attending the same professional associations or in general by interacting. According to Kaissi and Begun [31], fads are related to innovations, in terms of administrative technologies or models which

are imitated by organizations belonging to the same context, while fashion concerns the imitation of organizations belonging to other contexts.

- "Rational" adoption. When the decision to adopt the certification is driven by a real need to standardize procedures [32].

Figure 1 summarizes the above cited theoretical perspectives.

Taking a closer look, what is the contribution given by each theoretical paradigm to the explanation of the phenomenon of quality certification adoption?

Institutional theory states, (widely analyzed in chapter two), that organizations are prone to implement practices, procedures, or organizational designs, not only to achieve technical efficiency, but rather to appear legitimate to the external stakeholders [23-25]. Numerous studies have analyzed that organizations operating in the same context, are inclined to be similar. This phenomenon is caused by the impact of different pressures: mimetic, professional and coercive. In the case of Italian healthcare organizations, the need to introduce the ISO 9001 quality certification can be considered a legal constraint, for those hospitals which want to operate on behalf of the Italian Ministry of Health [33].

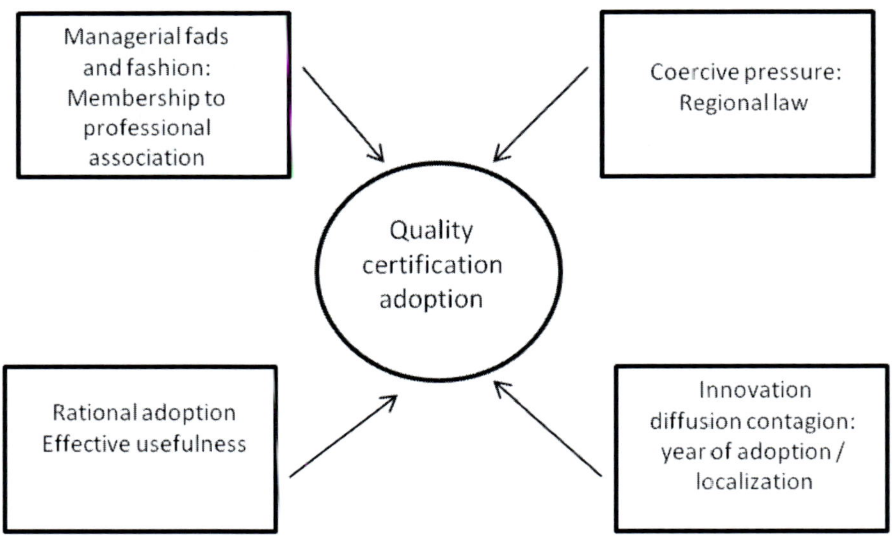

Figure 1. Quality certification adoption sources.

The term *contagion* is commonly used to indicate the diffusion of a disease caused by a close contact between individuals. Through an organizational perspective the term contagion indicates "*the diffusion of an idea or practice through a social system*" [27]. This theoretical approach looks at both the social events and the practical conditions which can lead to the contagion. The social contagion theory is frequently used to explain the transmission of thoughts, ideas or behaviors from one individual to a group of people. The same process occurs in the healthcare context, since a practice or an innovation emerges in a single organization, and it is progressively diffused in a large number of organizations. Often, a social contagion emerges from people belonging to the same social structure as a means to face the uncertainty of innovations [28]. Several theories were developed to explain the phenomenon considering the absence of a common idea about its cause [29]. The geographical proximity between the prior adopters and the later adopters is the first reason of contagion [27]. Gaba and Meyer [29] affirm that the higher the proximity between the source of contagion and "the influenced," the higher is the power of contagion. On this evidence Burt [28] offers a punctual explanation of the contagion, by distinguishing the cohesion and the structural equivalence as two motivations of its diffusion caused by the proximity between individuals (organizations). The diffusion can be caused by a frequent and empathic communication between the contagion source and the "influenced." By discussing about an innovation with other colleagues the awareness of it increases. Moreover, possible doubts and questions related to the topic can be shared and discussed by professionals. The contact between the contagion source and the "influenced" creates a sort of uniformity on the lens through which the innovation is observed. On the contrary, Burt [28] observes the presence of a structural equivalence, which shows that innovations are adopted not because of a maturation of a common opinion, but because of the competition between subjects (or organizations). Following this perspective, the organizations (individuals) are prone to adopt innovations if they perceive it as strategic in the competing field. In other words, the proximity between organizations represents the dimension in which cohesion and structural equivalence takes place. Further causes of the phenomenon seem to be related to the observation processes between organizations, which are responsible for the diffusion of the innovations [30].

In order to understand the phenomenon of social contagion two main characteristics of hospitals have been analyzed: the hospital's age and its size. Angst and colleagues [27] found that the older hospitals are, the greater the chance to intercept the diffusion of innovations among their peers. In addition, hospitals have more physicians that operate in other structures who are able to capture the new practices [34]. Therefore, we can expect teaching hospitals to be more prone to adopt innovations being larger than other healthcare structures. Even the age of hospitals is a significant variable to consider in the process of diffusion. The older the hospital, the higher the possibility that it is considered the "expert" structure in the innovations field.

Generally, the contagion theory is based on the awareness that practices, procedures and ideas become contagious within certain groups. Then, their diffusion becomes progressively irrational and organizations can easily start to operate as they would not normally. The process of contagion is not instantaneous and it happens through few steps.

First of all, a group of people (or organizations) focuses attention on the same subject (innovation, procedures, practice, organizational design). People (or organizations) progressively influence each other since they share that common focus. Starting from this moment, the conduct of people (or organizations) becomes irrational and the new idea progressively affects the group members.

The diffusion of both a practice and an innovation happens in correspondence with:

- Geographical proximity between individuals (or organizations);
- Opportunity of interaction between individuals (or organizations), due to the willingness to find social support to introduce the innovation and to the necessity to compete;
- Organizational features as size and age: the larger and older is the hospital, the more it is able to intercept innovations.

These conditions will be useful to interpret the results provided by the empirical analysis presented in the next paragraph.

The *managerial fads and fashion* theoretical approach indicates that organizations adopt a new model or practice as an information-based phenomenon. Under conditions of uncertainty, several organizations are prone to imitate those ones that are perceived as having superior information. In an economic perspective, the above tendency represents a rational approach to the question [31]. Although several authors have analyzed that phenomenon as a viral diffusion [35], generally managerial fashions have been conceived as "*management concepts that relatively speedily gain large shares in the public management discourse*" [36, 37]. They have been defined by Abrahamson [38] "*a relatively transitory collective belief disseminated by fashion setters, that a management technique leads to rational management progress.*" The analysis of this theoretical approach includes the need to determine the role of managerial rationality. Managers can decide to imitate an innovation or not, following their own knowledge, but also what the powerful organizations are doing [39].

Often, uncertain conditions lead managers to follow the "national fashion arena," which represents a fundamental concept in the innovation diffusion [35]. Madsen and Slatter [37] indicate what follows as examples of what is called "national fashion arena": consulting firms; software firms; management gurus; business school; conference organizers; business media; publisher/book editors; professional organizations; analysts and stakeholders; famous managers.

In this chapter the national fashion arena is represented by the membership of Italian hospitals to one of the main professional organizations in the healthcare context arena, which is the "Italian federation of healthcare organizations" (FIASO). The FIASO represents the majority of the trust hospitals, teaching hospitals and research hospitals operating within the Italian NHS. It appraises the participation and the active collaboration of members, through the use of working groups and the direct involvement of managers [40].

Membership to FIASO allows participants to keep in contact with professionals and managers belonging to the same context, even when the hospital's profile is different, which leads to the development of "managerial fads." Managerial fads occur for different reasons: the reduction of the ambiguity of the adopted innovations; the obtainment of legitimacy [18]; the willingness to reduce the competitive advantages of competitors by adopting their same innovations [41, 23-25, 42, 39]. Going into details, which organizations are commonly imitated? Scholars formulated numerous hypotheses about how the imitated organizations are chosen. We adopt the explanation provided by Abrahamson [39], who affirms that "*organizations that are poor in certain characteristics will imitate the adoption decisions of organizations that are rich in those characteristics.*" The empirical analysis provided in the next paragraph will prove this theoretical statement by showing that hospitals which are low in the case mix index (the case mix index indicates the complexity of patients treated), are prone to imitate those which are higher in it.

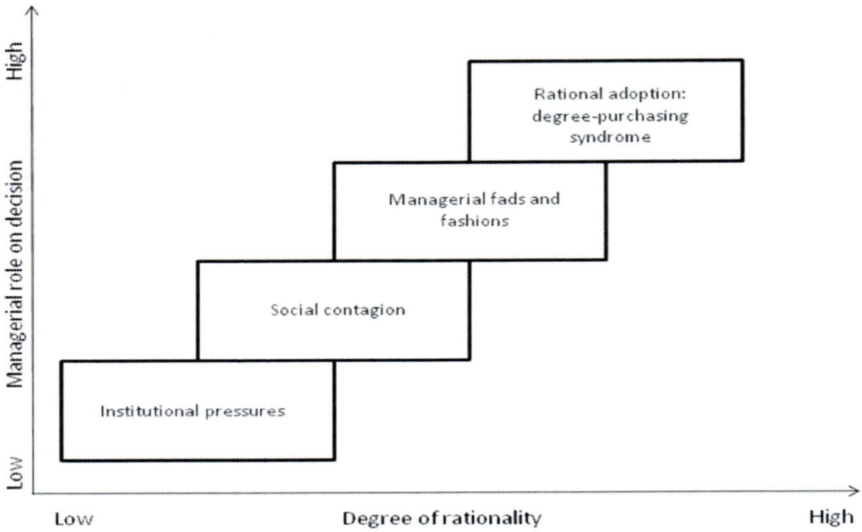

Figure 2. Four theoretical approaches on the adoption of quality certifications.

Finally, the most *"rational" perspective* on the issue affects those scholars that rejected the irrational interpretation of the diffusion of the quality certification recognizing that the process of adoption is very often "rational, neutral and unequivocal" [32]. Certain factors play a relevant role in promoting the decision to adopt the quality certification as a rational choice. Those factors are listed below: the social function of the certification is able to reinforce the stakeholder's trust in the organization [43]. The self-regulation effect [44, 45] and the legitimacy effect [46] conclude the list. Additionally, according to Boiral [32], the decision to adopt the quality certification is also influenced by the "degree-purchasing syndrome." It consists in the organizations' tendency to give priority to the production of documents and procedures, with the only aim to achieve the certification, without considering the benefits coming from the certification in itself. Just as those students who at university are interested not in the acquisition of knowledge, but in the obtainment of the degree, similarly organizations are interested in the achievement of the certification, more than in the acquisition of the quality oriented conducts [4, 47]. The above cited theoretical perspectives take into consideration different degrees of managerial impact on the decision to use the certification. The social contagion phenomenon and the spread of managerial fads and fashions will be analyzed taking into consideration the impact exerted by coercive pressures. The impact of managers is limited to the need to contrast uncertainty. Finally, in correspondence with the "rational" adoption, managerial willingness appears to be high.

Figure 2 provides a scheme of the four theoretical approaches, considering both the "Degree of rationality" and the degree of "Managerial role on the decision."

As Figure 2 shows, the higher the degree of rationality on the decision to adopt a quality certification, the stronger the managerial role in that decision.

The next section is dedicated to the explanation of the empirical evidence supplied on the process analyzed.

Analyzing the Spread of Quality Certifications in the Italian NHS

As previously stated, in order to analyze the phenomenon of the quality certifications adoption within the Italian NHS, we exploited the theoretical lenses already illustrated.

Methodology: Data Collection and Samples

Data used in this chapter comes from different sources. The first level of data collected concerns the list of certified Italian healthcare organizations, which comes from an international database. The aim of the database is to register all the certifications achieved by organizations belonging to any field all over the world. The database owner asked to remain anonymous. Data concerns the name and the object of quality certifications. Furthermore, it shows the geographical location of each organization, its institutional profile (Trust hospitals, Research hospitals, LHU's hospitals, Teaching hospitals) and the year in which the certification was obtained. Data about private hospitals was not considered since the study is limited to the public ones. Before starting the analysis we checked the general adoption rate of each region and we adjusted the results taking into consideration the number of hospitals. It allowed us to avoid considering the smallest regions as scarcely adopting.

A second level of data concerns the organizational features of the ISO 9001 certified healthcare organizations: in detail, the number of staffed beds and the complexity of the healthcare activities provided (ICM index). Data about the organizational features are available on the Italian Ministry of Health website [48].

The third level of data deals with the level of formalization of the regional health plans concerning the duty to introduce the ISO 9001 quality certification. Data was collected by performing a semantic analysis of the 21 more recent regional health plans within the Italian health system.

Table 2. Data and data sources

Dimension	Characteristics	Data collected	Source of data
ISO 9001 certification	Data concern a list of Italian healthcare organizations that have achieved the quality certification.	• Healthcare organizations name; • Object of the certification; • Geographical localization; • Institutional profile; • Year of the certification achievement;	International database (anonymous)
Structural features	Internal features of healthcare organizations belonging to the sample	• Number of staffed beds • ICM index	Website of the Italian Ministry of Health
Formalization of the prescription	Level of formalization about the duty to introduce a quality certification stated by the Italian regional health plans	• Low, medium, high level of formalization	Website of the Regional health authorities
Professional membership	Healthcare organizations membership to a professional healthcare association.	• Membership to the "Italian federation of healthcare organizations (FIASO)"	Web site of each certified healthcare organization

Finally, the last level of data considers whether or not organizations are members of the "Italian federation of healthcare organizations (FIASO)." Data was obtained by the analysis of the website of each certified healthcare organization. Table 2 summarizes data and its sources.

Data was collected from 125 Italian healthcare organizations certified by the ISO 9001. Among them 55% are trust hospitals, followed by 43% of LHU's hospitals, 14% of research hospitals and finally the last category is represented by teaching hospitals (12%).

When considering the geographical location, 70% of certified healthcare organizations are located in the north of Italy, followed by 18.4% which belong to the central area of Italy. Finally, 11.2% of the certified hospitals are located in the south of the country.

All the quality certifications surveyed were obtained between the 1999 and the 2014. 2002 was the year in which most of the quality certifications were achieved (23.2%).

RESULTS

This paragraph is dedicated to the presentation of the main results of the empirical analysis. The theoretical approaches analyzed in the previous pages of this chapter allow us to explain how and why healthcare organizations adopt quality certifications. We started from the analysis of the year of adoption, followed by the geographical location of the adopters, in order to demonstrate that a large number of adoptions may be explained as a phenomenon of social contagion among healthcare organizations.

Figure 3 represents the number of adoptions per year together with the size of the hospitals.

Firstly we note in Figure 3 the phenomenon of adoption of quality certifications started in 1999, as a consequence of managerial responsibilities attributed to hospital CEOs during the '90s. Thanks to the acquisition of the status of "trust," healthcare organizations started to pay considerable attention to the quality of care. Most of quality certifications were adopted between 1999 and 2002. The initial growth in the number of adoptions and its progressive decrease will be explained in detail afterwards. For what concerns the size of the adopters, both small and large hospitals can be considered "first adopters." Due to their size, smaller hospitals appear more flexible and able to introduce innovations. When the innovation implies a variation in the way in which the activities are performed, smaller hospitals show less resistance to changes, both through a structural and a procedural point of view. They are faster than large organizations in the implementation of innovations.

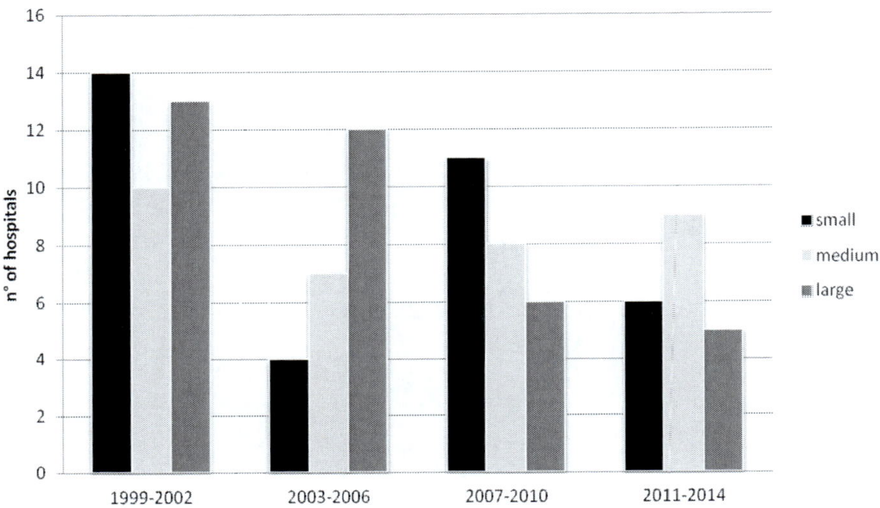

Figure 3. Year of adoption and size of adopters.

Even large healthcare organizations show a high level of adoption. It is due to the presence of a high number of professionals that thanks to their contact with the external environment, (for instance by attending professional workshops) are more prone to be exposed to innovations, which are in turn reported within their organizations. When the novelty of the quality certification ended (between the years 2003 and 2006), the number of quality certifications adopted by small organizations decreased. Contextually, large organizations continued to adopt following the need to face complexity through the use of standards in their daily activities. However, due to the uncertainty characterizing the healthcare context, the dynamic of adoption changed during the period between the years 2007 and 2010. As we can observe in Figure 3, small organizations again show a higher degree of adoption in comparison to the large ones. During this period, in the attempt to save resources, the Italian Ministry of Health progressively decided to close the smallest hospitals, especially where the appropriateness and the quality of the care were low. This is the most likely reason for the increase in quality certification adoption by small hospitals. In the same period, large healthcare organizations were progressively reducing their adoption rate following the contagion phenomenon trend. Finally, medium size organizations adopted a hybrid behavior being neither flexible enough to rapidly introduce the innovations, nor big enough to count on innovations coming from professionals' external experiences.

The decrease in adoptions that affected both small and large hospitals, in the last triennium, is a typical consequence of a diffusion originated by the contagion phenomenon.

It is confirmed in Figure 4, which provides the analysis of the dynamics of diffusion of quality certifications across the years.

We can observe a significant number of adoptions in 1999, followed by a rapid increase in 2002, when approximately 30 new certifications were adopted. The trend suddenly decreased in 2003 and it was stable between five and ten new adoptions per year, until 2014.

The confirmation of the typical S-shaped curve, which is a clear signal of contagion [28], comes from Figure 5 where the cumulative frequency of adopters is analyzed.

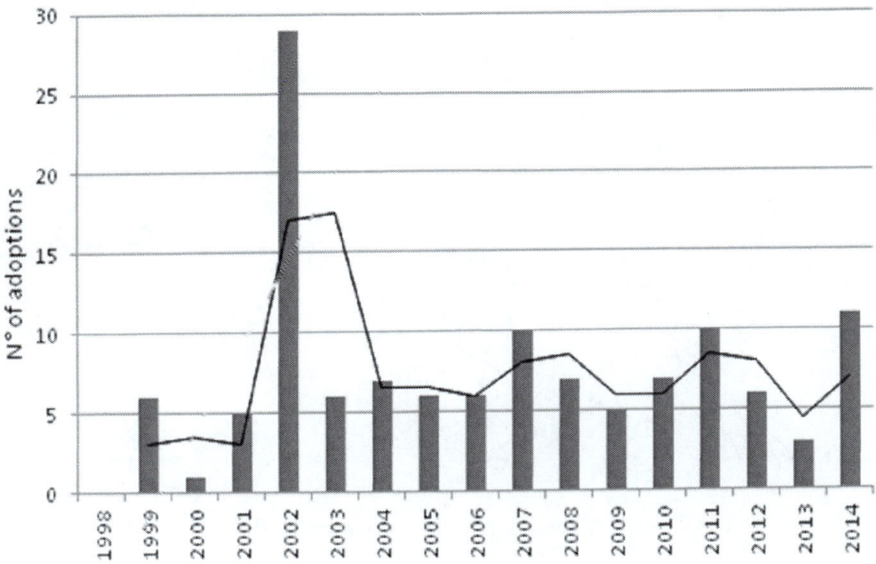

Figure 4. Year of adoption, general frequency.

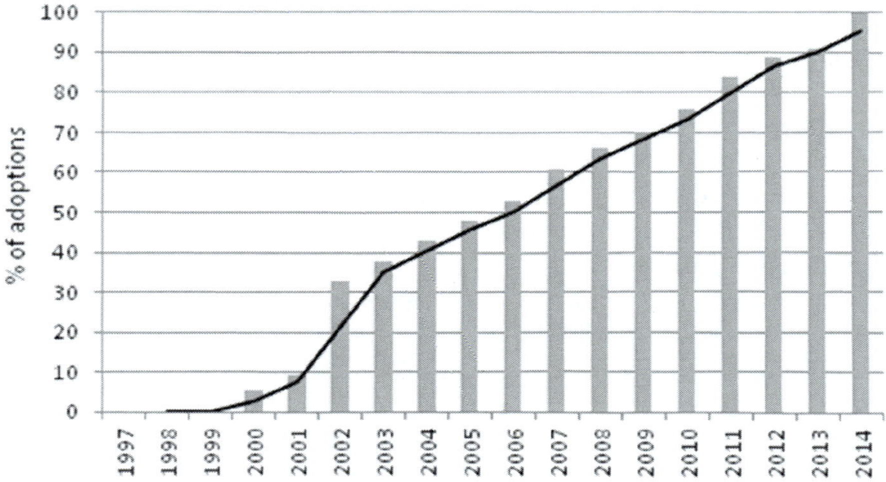

Figure 5. Diffusion of the adoptions.

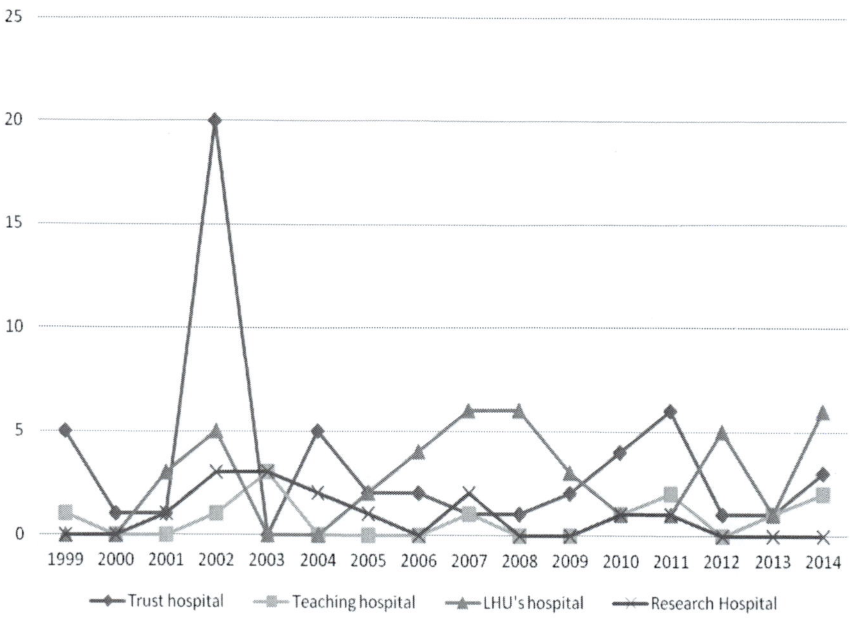

Figure 6. Annual adoption by institutional profiles of HCO.

Initially the number of adoptions is not high but as soon as the potential adopters start to be exposed to the innovation, there is a rapid increase in the adoption rate. Although the diffusion is at the maximum level in terms of rapidity of expansion, the number of adopting organizations gradually slows down, since they have already been adopted. From 2003 to 2014 the number of adoptions increased but with a lower rate than at the beginning of the process of diffusion.

Finally, in order to complete the analysis of the diffusion per year, it is interesting to identify which institutional profiles of the healthcare organizations are more affected by the contagion. Figure 6 shows the distribution of certifications per year with respect to the institutional profiles of the adopters.

Trust hospitals are the most inclined to adopt the innovation. Since the year 1999 they have represented the first institutional profile to adopt quality certifications, showing a peak during 2002. Excluding 2003, when new adoptions were not registered, in the following years the number of new certifications achieved by trust hospitals has remained stable between two and six per year. LHU hospitals can be considered the second adopters in terms of certifications achieved per year. In this case the trend started between the years 2000 and 2001. A first peak of five new adoptions characterized the year 2002, and the highest peak was between 2007 and 2008. It was replicated in 2014. Teaching hospitals and Research hospitals are the lowest adopters, showing a constant number of new adoptions per year (less than five units). This is counterintuitive considering what literature habitually affirms. We expected that due to both the size of the teaching hospitals, and the opportunity of their professionals to attend workshops and meetings, they would be the highest adopters.

Considering the social contagion theory approach, it is now necessary to evaluate both the geographical proximity between the adopters and the timing of the adoption. Our evidence proves that the higher the proximity between the "influenced" and the source of contagion, the higher the chance of contagion. Consequently, the geographical proximity determines the mimicry between organizations. Organizations that are located in the same area compete for the same resources and customers, and therefore they are prone to adopt similar innovations. The results of that process are visible in Figure 7.

Except for five organizations (4% of the sample), which autonomously adopted the quality certifications, the remaining healthcare organizations are concentrated in few regional areas. This is the case of Lombardy, Piedmont, Veneto and Emilia Romagna, but also Latium and Campania. The major concentration of adopters is located in close regions, showing two extended areas of adopters (marked by black circles). In this section, we focus on the factor of proximity between adopters, without considering alternative explanations of the phenomenon, such as, the institutional pressures, which will be analyzed afterwards.

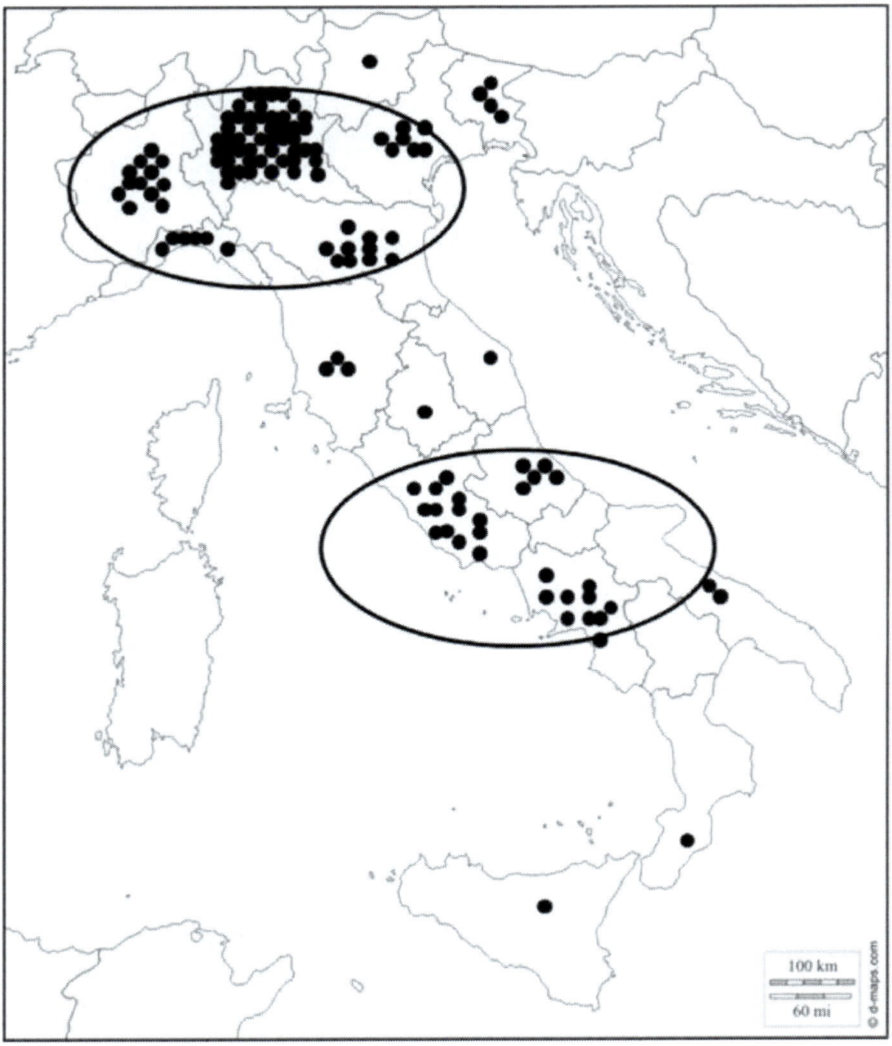

Figure 7. Geographical location of certified adopters.

Two questions emerge from Figure 7. What is the relation between geographical proximity and timing of adoption? When did the contagion affect the different regional areas? The answer is that organizations situated in close regions, move for the first adoption in the same period due to competitiveness. When the temporal difference of adoption between competing organizations is too long, non-adopters may be disadvantaged. By analyzing Figure 8 it is possible to notice that the moment of the first adoption is similar in all geographical areas.

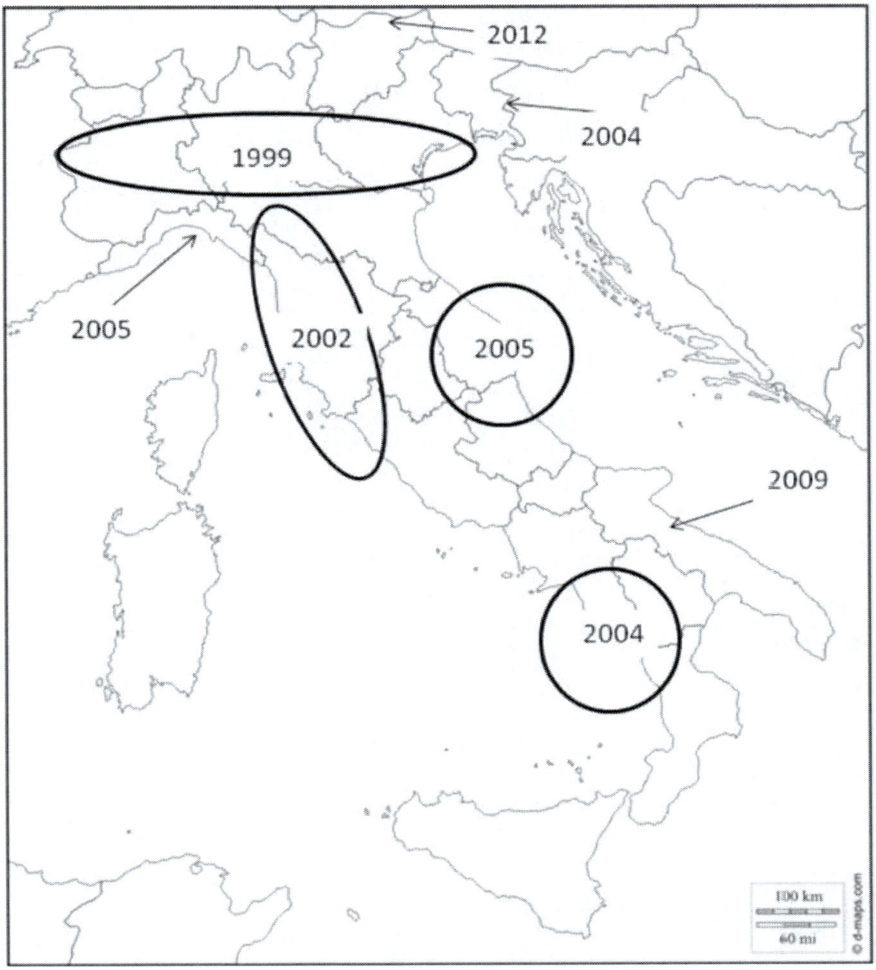

Figure 8. Geographical proximity of adopters and year of first adoption.

The first adoption experiences are located in three nearby regions: Piedmont, Lombardy and Veneto, where 3 quality certifications have been introduced during 1999. In 2002, the same phenomenon affected the close areas of: Emilia Romagna, Tuscany and Latium. In 2004, it happened for the regions of Campania and Calabria, and in 2005 for the regional areas of Marche, Abruzzi and Umbria. In addition, Figure 8 shows that there are some residual regional areas where the decision to introduce the quality certification has occurred independently of the nearby areas and with a different timing.

Table 3. Actors involved in the diffusion of quality certifications: A general view

	N° HCO adopters	Year of first adoption	Level of formalization of the law	% of adopters belonging to professional associations
Piedmont	11	1999	Medium	100
Valle d'Aosta	0	-	Low	-
Lombardy	49	1999	High	20
Liguria	6	2005	Medium	83
Aut. P. of Trento	1	2012	Low	0
Aut. P. of Bolzano	0	-	Low	-
Veneto	7	1999	Low	0
Friuli Venetia Giulia	4	2004	Medium	25
Emilia Romagna	10	2002	High	40
Tuscany	3	2002	Low	0
Umbria	1	2005	High	100
Marche	1	2005	Medium	100
Abruzzi	5	2005	Low	20
Molise	0	-	Low	-
Latium	13	2002	Low	0
Campania	10	2004	Low	30
Basilicata	0	-	Low	-
Puglia	2	2009	Low	0
Calabria	1	2004	High	0
Sicily	1	-	Low	100
Sardinia	0	-	Low	-

It means that the contagion phenomenon theory is not sufficient to explain the whole phenomenon of adoption; therefore it is necessary to introduce other theoretical elements to complete the analysis. Table 3 shows how new elements, such as the institutional coercive pressures and managerial fashions are distributed within Italian regions.

Table 3 shows the number of adopters and the year in which the first quality certification was adopted in each regional area, together with the level of formalization of the regional laws and membership of a professional healthcare association.

As Table 3 proves only a few Italian regions show a medium level of formalization of the law concerning the quality in the healthcare service provision, while 4 regions display a high level of formalization. Most of the Regions show a low level of formalization. It means that their choice to adopt a quality certification is not strictly related to the need to fulfill legal requests. The last column shows the percentage of adopters belonging to professional associations in each region. Figure 9 provides a graphic representation of the coercive pressure exerted by the law formalization. In addition it shows the geographical location of the adopters and the level of formalization of regional laws. Bold circles indicate high formalization, grey circles correspond to a medium level of formalization, and dotted circles indicate a low level of formalization.

As Figure 9 shows that the dynamic of adoption does not always follow the law coercion which is not the only reason on which the diffusion of the quality certification is based. Despite the circumstance where a high level of law formalization corresponds a large number of adopters (Lombardy and Emilia Romagna), there are several regions where there is not a direct correspondence, (Umbria, and Calabria). On the contrary, in the Piedmont region where the level of law formalization is medium, the adopters are numerous. Finally, in several cases, despite the low formalization of the law, (Latium, Campania, Veneto and Abruzzi), data show a discrete number of adopters.

As it was for the contagion theory the parallelism between law coercion and adoptions is not adequate to explain the whole phenomenon of adoption. Several healthcare organizations decided to adopt the quality certification without following a compulsory directive. Membership in professional associations is the next element to be analyzed to have a proper analysis of the phenomenon.

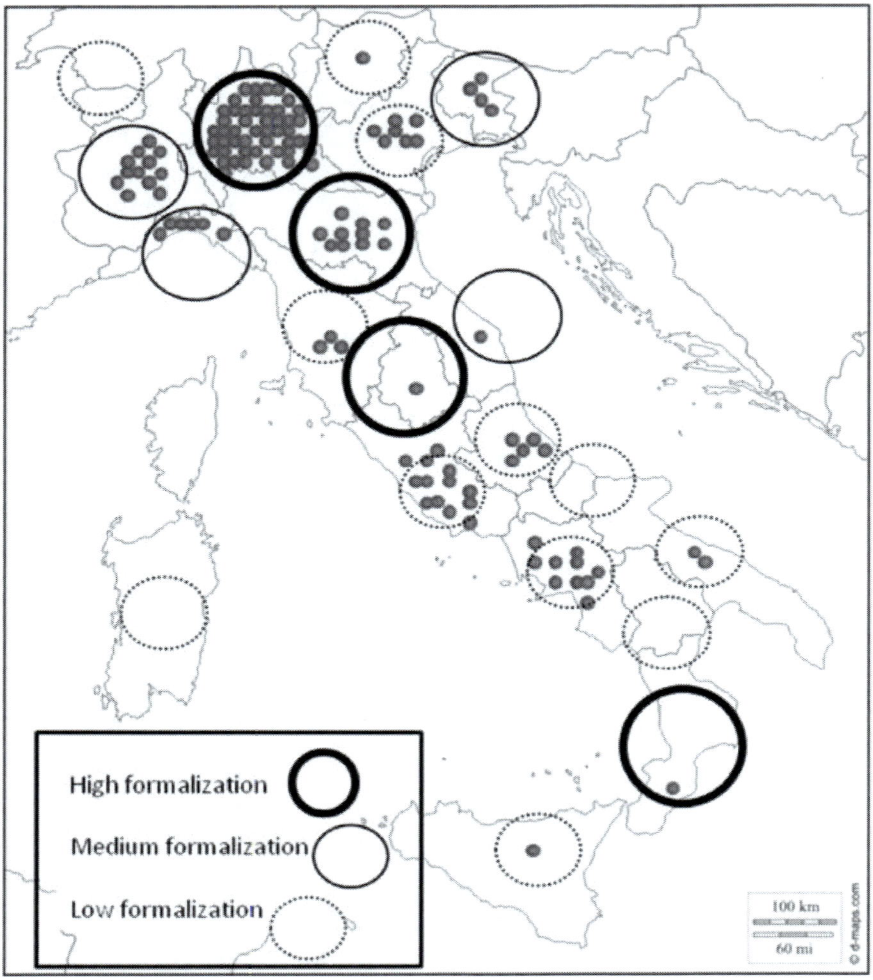

Figure 9. Adopters and levels of law formalization.

Membership in professional associations represents one of the main vehicles of diffusion of managerial fashions. Professional associations allow managers and professionals belonging to different healthcare organizations to keep in contact by attending the same meetings and seminars. Through the transmission of information, managerial fashions are shared and then followed. Figure 10 maps the geographical distribution of the adopters who are members of FIASO professional associations (full dots).

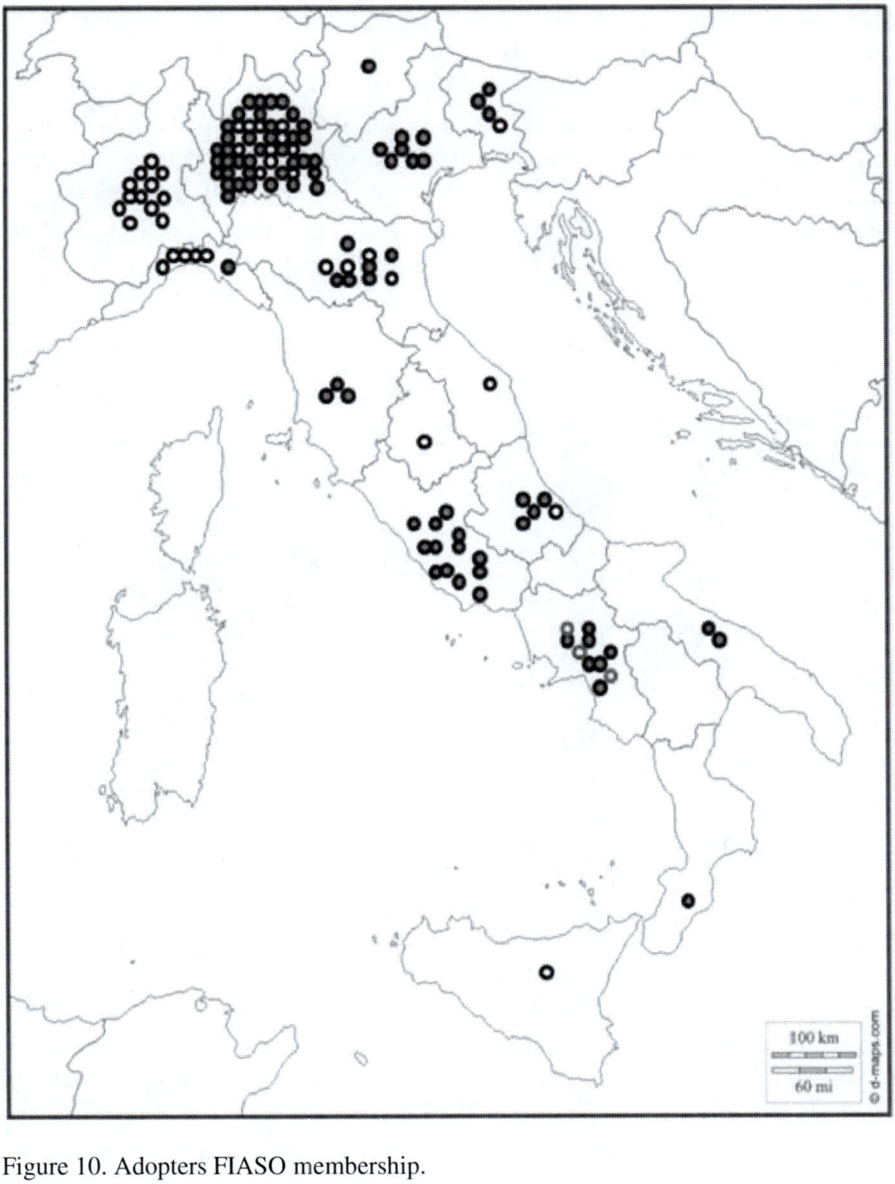

Figure 10. Adopters FIASO membership.

FIASO is a voluntary based association of healthcare organizations whose aim is to collect experiences and to share information for the benefit of members. The degree of adherence to national associations or to regional ones is a voluntary choice of the healthcare organization. We may suppose that when the regional association is perceived as more useful than the national one, the degree of association to the FIASO decreases. We decided to measure the degree of association to the FIASO, because it offers a similar pattern of information to all the members independently of their geographical location.

In most cases there is a correspondence between the decision to introduce the quality certification and the membership to the "Italian federation of healthcare organizations (FIASO)," which means that the association may be the tool used for the transmission of the ideas [37].

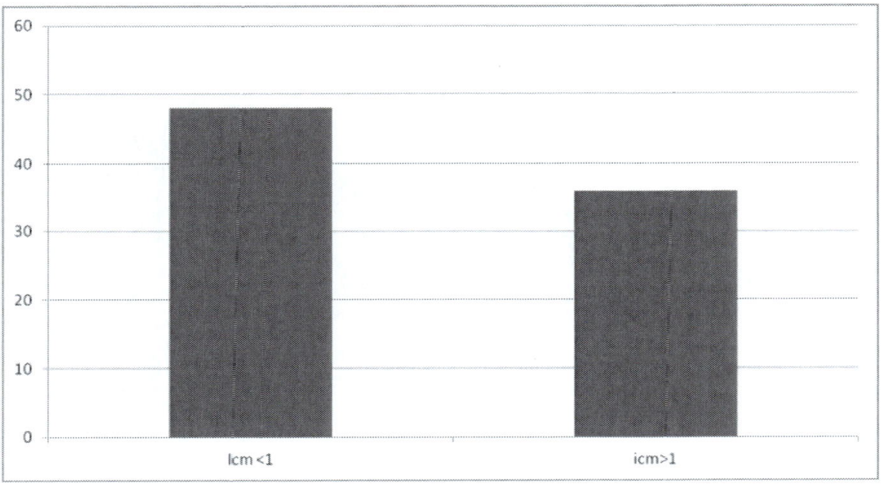

Figure 11. Level of case mix of adopters.

Membership in professional associations is not the only vehicle to transmit managerial fashions. Often professionals are prone to imitate the behavior of "powerful organizations," managers [31] who are identified as the best performers. In the discipline of standards, a group of appreciated standard supporters is able to attract new members [11]. In this research, powerful healthcare organizations have been identified through their case mix index by analyzing the presence of a level of case mix greater than 1. It represents the critical threshold to indicate the complexity of the patients treated. We tried to identify where the "powerful organizations" adopters are located, thus investigating if the phenomenon of adoption can be recognized as a managerial imitation. First of all, Figure 11 shows that the minority of the organizations belonging to the sample presents a case mix index greater than 1. Figure 12 on the other hand shows where powerful organizations are located.

In almost all the Italian regions there is a "powerful organization" among the adopters which means that the decision to introduce the quality certification can be influenced by a managerial choice of imitating those organizations.

An exception to this behavior is seen in the autonomous province of Trento, and the regions of Puglia and Calabria where the diffusion of managerial fads does not represent the correct quality certification diffusion explanation.

Figure 12. Presence of powerful organizations among adopters.

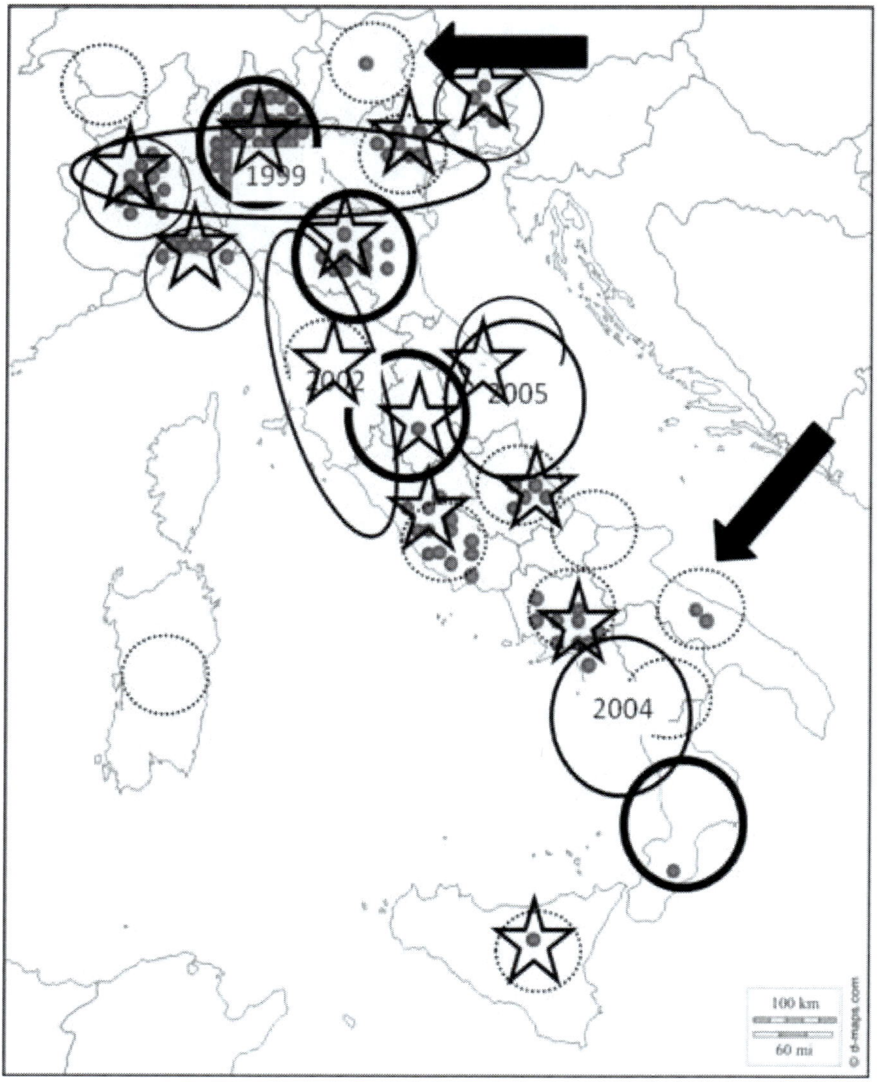

Figure 13. Quality certification rational adoptions.

As we previously stated, we expected a few residual adopters whose behavior cannot be explained through the neo-institutional theory, nor by the contagion phenomenon or by the diffusion of managerial fads and fashions. The behavior of the residual adopters is “rationally based” and it concerns the decision to adopt quality certifications following real organizational needs. In our sample this circumstance concerns those organizations in which the quality certification adoptions are not similar to the remaining ones in terms of year of adoption, nor are they based on the isomorphism mechanisms nor on the spread of managerial fashions.

Figure 13 reports two cases marked by black arrows, in which it is possible to recognize a "rational adoption" of the quality certification.

According to Boiral [32], few organizations have adopted ISO standards with the clear purpose of improving internal practices [4, 47, 49]. We can suppose that if at the beginning their initial purpose was driven by the willingness to obtain certification, during the procedure of certification, they developed a real interest in improving the internal practices through its introduction.

Beyond a doubt, we can affirm that the phenomenon of diffusion of quality certifications is extremely complex and it needs to be explained through several theoretical approaches.

DISCUSSION

How do managers face uncertainty? In the attempt to provide an empirical explanation to this question, we have focused on the motivations and the pattern of diffusion of the quality certifications among Italian healthcare organizations. The choice of analyzing the quality certification derives from the strategic role exerted by standardization on healthcare organizations. Through the use of standards, organizations are able to know how and why activities have to be accomplished. Moreover, besides being the most popular standard around the world, the quality certification concerns one of the main relevant aspects of the healthcare service provision. Many Italian healthcare organizations progressively obtained the certification after the '90s when numerous normative interventions occurred. Then the quality certification started to be considered an innovation and therefore the dynamics behind its diffusion have become the object of analysis. The four dominant theoretical lenses on the diffusion of an innovation have been analyzed, and then tested through empirical analysis.

As demonstrated, the decision to introduce quality certifications arises from the coexistence of certain circumstances on which the previously listed theoretical approaches are based:

- The law prescription. According to Powell and Di Maggio [23-24] and Meyer and Rowan [25], if a coercive pressure exists in a context, the organizations belonging to it will tend to become isomorphic by adopting the rule in the attempt to obtain legitimacy. In our context the achievement of the quality certification, for several regions, is an obligation to be met in order to provide healthcare services on the behalf of the Italian NHS.
- Social proximity. According to Angst and colleagues [27], it is denoted by a hospital's membership to a regional health system. The geographical location and the temporal lag of adoption seem to be two relevant dimensions to be examined. The Italian NHS can be considered a national healthcare system composed of various regional healthcare arrangements. For that reason, it is interesting to analyze how and when the diffusion occurred.
- The membership in a professional association according to Kaissi and Begun [31] and with Madsen [37] is one of the “actors” responsible for the diffusion of managerial fashions. During the past years in Italy a series of hospitals federations and associations have been established, giving professionals and managers the opportunity to share experiences and knowledge. In addition to that, according to Kaissi and Begun, [31], the presence of powerful organizations among the adopters is the reason why managerial fads started to be diffused. It is because organizations tend to imitate the adoption decisions of those organizations that are perceived as successful. According to our sample, it seems that a higher level of the complexity of healthcare services provided, corresponds a positive and successful perception of the work.
- The presence of “residual” organizations, for which none of the previous theoretical lenses seem to be applicable. According to Boiral [32] those organizations adopt the quality certification for a real need. The presence in our sample of healthcare organizations, which are not influenced by the constraints of law, nor by the social proximity to others, or by the attempt to imitate a powerful organization, allows us to hypothesize that the decision to adopt is related to the willingness to modify internal practices.

The evidence presented in this chapter proves that often the decision to achieve the quality certification occurs by following an S-shaped curve of diffusion, thus indicating the presence of a social contagion between organizations. In a general perspective, we have found that the decision made by early adopters was predominantly rational, while the followers can be considered the ones who imitate organizations [31]. In our sample the imitating organizations are mainly medium size hospitals, for which the adopting rate increases through the years, thereby the contagion phenomenon occurred because of the structural characteristics of early adopters. According to Angst [27], when the adoption is done by a small hospital it is big news, while it is not when a large hospital is involved. It seems clear that professionals are responsible for diffusing ideas and knowledge. But how does the process of diffusion occur? Does it occur when professionals are members of the same associations, or because they observe what managers of famous hospitals are doing? Managerial fashion and fads are among the drivers of the diffusion of innovations. They are not related to the proximity between organizations, but rather to a contact between managers. In both cases, the contact between managers determines the diffusion of ideas and innovations.

Several adopting hospitals of the research sample are members of the “Italian federation of healthcare organizations (FIASO).” Thanks to the use of newsletters, meetings, or seminars, managers have the opportunity to interact. On the other hand, our results show that in almost all regions, it is possible to recognize a “powerful organization” among the adopters. By observing what the powerful organizations are doing, and by miming their decisions, managers accept the innovation and consequently they make its diffusion possible.

What happens when the innovation is indicated by the law? According to the neo institutional approach, all the organizations which are submitted to a legal constraint decide to adopt the innovation in order to appear legitimate. The research results are counter intuitive. It is because in a few cases there is a correspondence between the level of formalization of the law and the necessity to adopt the quality certifications, while in the majority of them there is no correspondence. In addition we found that in several regions, where the level of obligation is low, the adoption rate is high.

Although interesting results were provided, this chapter does not allow us to analyze whether the obtainment of the certification has really changed the way in which healthcare activities are performed, or if it is just another example of decoupling [22]. Moreover, the points of view of professionals and patients should be taken into consideration to evaluate the quality certification efficiency. The organization’s conduct exerts an inevitable impact on the organizational behavior of professionals; therefore it is useful to survey the employees' opinion and satisfaction about the introduction of the ISO 9001 quality certification.

Despite the above cited limitations, the evidence provided offers some significant indications to both managers and policy makers.

Managers should try to understand the role of the innovation and its benefits avoiding a mere imitation of successful experiences or a passive accomplishment of the legal prescriptions. Policy-makers should pay attention to the adoption phenomenon even for hospitals located in regions where the legal imposition is low. The hospital's policy makers should measure performances before and after the introduction of standardization tools trying to understand their outcomes. Furthermore, it may be necessary to make certification a formal requirement for all healthcare organizations, considering the significant role that can be exerted by the government in the process of certification [33].

CONCLUSION

Chapter three provides an explanation of the diffusion of the ISO 9001 quality certification within the Italian healthcare organizations, by following different theoretical perspectives of analysis. Despite some limitations, this chapter offers interesting results. The first limitation is that being the analysis country-based the research is not exploitable on a large scale. What we observed is the dynamic of diffusion of the ISO 9001 quality certification in a confined sector i.e., healthcare, which is characterized by peculiar features. Moreover, the Italian healthcare system shows different features in terms of obligation of quality certification, when compared with other national health systems. Nevertheless, the theoretical approaches adopted in this chapter can be exported in all sectors and in all national systems, in the attempt to explain the diffusion processes. The second limitation is related to the healthcare organization's will to make public the certification achievement or not. However, since we know that the presence of a certification is considered a source of legitimacy, we can suppose that organizations are more prone to publicize its adoption rather than hide it.

Despite the above mentioned limitations, chapter three offers an interesting attempt at interpreting the dynamic of diffusion of standardization. Moreover, it provides an accurate study on the way in which it can affect healthcare service provision and a clear example of how managers can deal with uncertainty.

REFERENCES

[1] Mascia, Daniele, Federica Morandi, and Americo Cicchetti. 2014. "Hospital restructuring and physicians job satisfaction: an empirical study." *Health policy*, 114: 118-127.

[2] Sandholtz, Kurt W. 2012. "Making standards stick: a theory of coupled vs decoupled compliance." *Organization studies*, 33: 655.

[3] Beck, Nikolaus, and Peter Walgenbach. 2005. "Technical efficiency or adaptation to institutional expectations? The adoption of ISO 9000 standards in the German mechanical engineering industry." *Organization studies*, 26: 841-866.

[4] Boiral, Oliver. 2003. "*ISO 9000: Outside the iron cage*." Organization Science, 14: 720–737.

[5] Brunsson, Nils, and Bengt Jacobsson. 2000. "The contemporary expansion of standardization." In *A world standards* edited by Nils Brunsson, and Bengt Jacobsson, 1-17. Oxford: Oxford University Press.

[6] Daft, Richard.L. 2007. *Organizzazione Aziendale*. Apogeo (in Italian).

[7] Cicchetti, Americo. 2004. *La progettazione Organizzativa*. Franco Angeli sanità (in Italian).

[8] Botzem, Sebastian, and Leonhard Dobusch. 2012. "Standardization cycles: A process perspective on the formation and diffusion of transnational standards." *Organization Studies*, 33(5/6): 737-762.

[9] Kerwer Dieter. 2005. "Rules that many use: standards and global regulation." *Governance*, 18: 611-632.

[10] Slager, Rieneke. Jean-Pascal Gond and Jeremy Moon. 2012. "Standardization as institutional work: the regulatory power of a responsible investment standard." *Organization studies*, 33 (5-6): 763-790.

[11] Van den Ende, Jan, Geerten van de Kaa, Simon den Uijl and Henk J. de Vries. 2012. "The paradox of standard flexibility: the effects of co-evolution between standard and interorganizational network." *Organization studies*, 33 (5-6): 705-736.

[12] Ministry of health, Bhutan. 2011. *Quality assurance and standardization manual*. Quality assurance and standardization division.

[13] Guler, Isin, Mauro F. Guillén and John Muir Macpherson. 2002. "Global competition, institutions and the diffusion of organizational practices:

the international spread of ISO 9000 quality certificates." *Administrative science quarterly*, 47 (2): 202: 232.

[14] ISO, 2014. http://www.iso.org/iso/home.htm.

[15] ISO, 2013. *Survey on adoption*. ISO.

[16] Greene, Andrew H. 1991. "ISO 9000: Globalizing quality standards." *Production and inventory management*, September: 74-75.

[17] Motwani, Jaideep, Chun Hung Cheng, and Manu S. Madan. 1997. "Implementation of ISO 9000 in the healthcare sector." *Health marketing quarterly*, 14 (2): 63-72.

[18] Fikru, Mahelet G. 2014. "International certification in developing countries: the role of internal and external institutional pressures." *Journal of environmental management*, 144: 286-296.

[19] Sauder, Michael and Wendy Nelson Espeland. 2009. "The discipline of rankings: tight coupling and organizational change." *American sociological review*, 74: 62-82.

[20] ISO Management Systems magazine. http://www.iso.org/ims.

[21] Edelman, Lauren B. 1992. "Legal ambiguity and symbolic structures: organizational mediation of civil rights law." *American Journal of Sociology*, 97: 1531-1576.

[22] Mascia Daniele, Federica Morandi, and Americo Cicchetti. 2014. "Looking Good or Doing Better? Patterns of Decoupling in the Implementation of Clinical Directorates." *Health Care Management Review,* 39(2):111-123, April/June.

[23] Powell, Walter and Paul Di Maggio. 1983. "The iron cage revisited: institutional isomorphism and collective rationality in organizational field." *American sociological review*, 48(2): 147-160.

[24] Powell, Walter and Paul Di Maggio. 1991. *The new institutionalism in organizational analysis*. Chicago: University of Chicago press.

[25] Meyer, John W. and Brian Rowan. 1977. "Institutionalized Organizations: Formal Structure as Myth and Ceremony." *American Journal of Sociology*, 83: 340-363.

[26] Helms, Wesley, and Karnagan Webb. 2014. "Perceived voluntary code legitimacy: towards a theoretical framework and research agenda." *Journal of management and organization*, 20 (3): 287-312.

[27] Angst, Corey, Ritu Agarwal, Samba V. Murthy, and Ken Kelley. 2010. "Social contagion and information technology diffusion: the adoption of electronic medical records in U.S. hospitals." *Management Science*, 56 (8): 1219-1241.

[28] Burt, Ronald S. 1987. "Social contagion and innovation: cohesion versus structural equivalence." *American Journal of sociology*, 92 (6): 1287-1335.

[29] Gaba, Vibha, and Alan D. Meyer A. 2008. "Crossing the organizational species barrier: how venture capital practices infiltrated the information technology sector." *Academy of management journal*, 51: 976-998.

[30] Strang, David, and Sarah A. Soule. 1998. "Diffusion in organizations and social movements: from hybrid corn to poison pills." *Annual review of sociology*, 24: 265-290.

[31] Kaissi Amer A., and James W. Begun. 2008. "Fads, fashions, and bandwagons in healthcare strategy." *Healthcare management review*, 33 (2): 94-102.

[32] Boiral, Olivier. 2012. "ISO certificates as organizational degrees? Beyond the rational myths of the certification process." *Organization studies*, 33(5-6): 633-654.

[33] Lee, Brandon H. 2009. "The infrastructure of collective action and policy content diffusion in the organic food industry." *Academy of management journal*, 52 (6): 1247-1269.

[34] Pisano, Gary, Richard Bohemer, and Amy C. Edmonson. 2001. "Organizational differences in rates of learning: evidence from the adoption of minimally invasive cardiac surgery." *Management Science*, 47: 752-768.

[35] Røvik, Kjell Arne. 2011. "From fashion to virus: an alternative theory of organizations' handling of management ideas." *Organization studies*, 32: 631-653.

[36] Jung, Nicole, and Alfred Kieser A., 2012. "Consultants in the management fashion arena." In *The Oxford handbook of management consulting*, edited by Matthias Kipping and Timothy Clark, 327-346. New York: Oxford University Press.

[37] Madsen, Dag Øivind, and Kåre Slåtten. 2013. "The role of the management fashion arena in the cross national diffusion of management concepts: the case of the balanced scorecard in the Scandinavian countries." *Administrative science*, 3: 110-142.

[38] Abrahamson, Eric. 1996. "Management fashion." *Academy of management review*, 21 (1): 254-285.

[39] Abrahamson, Eric. 1991. "Managerial fads and fashions: the diffusion and rejection of innovations." *Academy of management review*, 16 (3): 586-612.

[40] Fiaso website: http://www.fiaso.it/.
[41] Rogers, Everett M. 1983. *Diffusion of the innovation*. (2nd edition). New York Press.
[42] Abrahamson, Eric, and Lori Rosenkopf. 1993. "Institutional and Competitive Bandwagons: Using Mathematical Modeling as a Tool to Explore Innovation Diffusion." *The Academy of Management Review*, 18 (3): 487-517.
[43] Gendrom, Yves, Roy Suddaby R., and Helen Lam. 2006. "An examination of the ethical commitment of professional accountants to auditor independence." *Journal of business ethic*, 64: 169-193.
[44] Christmann, Petra, and GlenTaylor. 2006. "Firm self- regulation through international certifiable standards: determinants of symbolic versus substantive implementation." *Journal of international business studies*, 37: 863-878.
[45] Prakash, Aseem, and Matthew Potosky. 2007. "Collective action through voluntary environmental programs: a club theory perspective." *Policy studies journal*, 35: 773-792.
[46] Martin Roger D. 2007. "Through the ethics looking glass: another view of the world of auditors and ethics." *Journal of business ethics*, 70: 5-14.
[47] Boiral, Oliver. 2007. "Corporate greening through ISO 14001: A rational myth?" *Organization Science*, 18, 127–146.
[48] Italian Ministry of health website: http://www.ministerosalute.org.
[49] Walgenbach, Peter. 2001. "The production of distrust by a means of producing trust." *Organization Studies*, 22: 693–714.

Chapter 4

COMMON INSIDE CHALLENGES: LOOKING FOR ORGANIZATIONAL AND INDIVIDUAL WORK VALUES CONGRUENCE

ABSTRACT

Within the healthcare sector, employee job satisfaction plays an important role in determining good levels of performance, due to the direct influence on quality and appropriateness of care. Literature confirms that job satisfaction tends to be higher in those contexts in which a reasonable degree of coherence between individual and organizational values occur. By using data on 2597 doctors and nurses staffed in 28 Italian hospitals, the effect of work values congruence on employee satisfaction has been demonstrated. In addition gender, age and job role of surveyed employees have been recognized as being responsible for work values alignment. Managerial implications have been demonstrated.

Keywords: work values, job satisfaction, performance measurement

INTRODUCTION

In the analysis of the hospital challenges the role of the congruence between individual and organizational work values is fundamental, due to its effect on employee satisfaction. Work values can be defined as "*the outcomes people desire and feel should they attain through work*" [1; p. 1121], in other words they are the values that people wish to find in their work environment [2, 3]. Work values represent the main characteristics of a desirable workplace [4, 6]. They directly influence various aspects of individual behavior such as problem-solving and judgment skills [1, 7], propensity for conflict, frequency and intensity of communication, career choices [8-10], job performance [3] and job satisfaction. Job satisfaction is not only associated with work values but also with the opinion that individuals have about their working conditions [11].

Scholars have identified different types of work values that are based on intrinsic, extrinsic, social, and status dimension of work [1, 5-7, 12-16]. According to Hertzberg's definition of work [17], intrinsic work values are related to the content of the work performed e.g., learning opportunities, autonomy, responsibility, and to the opportunity to exercise creativity and initiative [1]. Extrinsic work values are instead related to the outcomes and to the tangible recognition of individual work. They are commonly represented by salary or career advancement. Further distinctions can be made in the work values analysis. The status-related work values, which concern prestige and involvement within the workplace, together with the influence in decision-making processes. Finally, the social-related work values category that is the set of values related to the relational component of a work position e.g., organizational climate, altruistic behavior, and care of colleagues [6, 18]. It has been documented that individuals show different levels of appreciation for those categories of work values. It depends on both a wide range of individual and professional characteristics (personality, etc.), and the perception that the individual has of his/her working environment in relation to the professional dimensions that he/she considers the most important [8, 3, 18-21, 9].

Although many authors consider work values as a stable trait of personality, the results of a meta-analysis conducted by Jin and Rounds [6] documented that, "*within each life stage, individuals may set priorities for different values according to their experiences (p. 328),*" learning them from parents, teachers, friends, colleagues [22, 23]. Major changes in work values appreciation may happen in correspondence to particular family events [24], such as a wedding or the birth of children [24-27], or according to experiences or changes in working conditions [11, 28, 26, 24]. Those changes can occur because of two different processes recognized as "*acclimation or compensation*" to the working circumstances.

Acclimation indicates the tendency of employees to give more importance to those values that they find within the professional environment. The compensation process describes how individuals tend to prioritize those values, which are not satisfied within their own organizational context [6, 11].

For instance, well-paid workers and members of high social classes tend to take for granted the extrinsic dimension of their work, giving more importance to its intrinsic dimension, even when the latter is satisfied. On the contrary, workers in precarious economic conditions tend to take a greater interest in the extrinsic aspects of their work.

The importance of work values within organizations can be analyzed from both the employee's and the organization's point of view. Based on Schneider's approach [29], employee behavior during their career is driven by the attraction- selection- attrition model. An individual is prone to choose and to be selected by those organizations that share with him goals and values. On the contrary, whenever the organizations' values and beliefs are different from those of the employee, he/she will be prone to leave the organization, due to the attrition.

Consequently, organizations are progressively composed of individuals characterized by similar values.

From an organizational point of view, although an excessive similarity between colleagues can determine negative effects e.g., the *groupthink* phenomenon [30], the creation of a general common sense across employees allows the achievement of an alignment between individual and organizational values [22]. Moreover, it can affect the minimization of the costs of turnover and promote the extra- roles behaviors [31, 32]. As the next paragraph shows work values congruence may generate also important effects in terms of productivity and satisfaction within the workplace.

Individual and Organizational Work Values Congruence

Scholars have recognized an important role in the congruence between individual and organizational values. In their opinion, congruence leads to an improvement of employee attitudes and behaviors [33]. In correspondence to the "*similarity between values held by individuals and organizations*" [34, p.655], a perfect fit [33, 35, 22], able to affect employees' happiness and comfort [36], occurs. The fit concerns different levels such as person-job, person-organization, person- group and person- supervisor [37]. The presence of the fit can be considered the base to interpret some organizational behaviors such as the choice of a workplace or the employees' performance. Among the existing fittings, the person- group fit is particularly interesting due to the role played within healthcare organizations. The person-group fit is based on goals sharing and values sharing able to affect job satisfaction and organizational commitment [37], but also individuals' attitudes, behaviors and performances [38, 29, 22].

About the existing impact of values congruence on organizations, Edward and Cable [34] provide a relevant contribution, by identifying four dimensions that value congruence may positively affect: *Communication, Predictability, Attraction* and *Trust*. In the presence of value congruence, *Communication* between organizational members will result more fluent, frequent and effective. The ability to *Predict* decisions and events will increase [39]. Employees will be interested in avoiding conflicts and sharing tasks and procedures, thus increasing the *Attraction* of similar members. Finally, the *Trust* in principles and goals of the organization will increase [40], making the decision-making processes more rapid.

As a whole, the effect of work values congruence on the above-cited dimensions determines the improvement of the coordination between colleagues. It is of quintessential importance within healthcare organizations where the quality of the services provided deeply depends on the effectiveness of the coordination mechanisms.

In the next subsections, we will demonstrate how work values improve the organizational dimensions indicated by Edward and Cable [34].

Value Congruence and Communication

Within the healthcare organizations, as we have already seen, the value congruence between individual and organization may improve the quality of the *Communication*. A good level of communication between physicians, nurses, allied health staff and patients is a crucial factor both to improve work scheduling and to increase patient satisfaction. Communication tools may be both formal, such as scheduled meetings or guidelines, and informal, for example direct contacts, unplanned meetings or IT tools. Although the informal communication tools are cheaper than the formal ones, they are considered the most effective [41]. It is especially observed within healthcare organizations, where the direct contact between actors is fundamental for patient care [42]. Besides the organization's needs, the implementation of the informal communication tools is based on the organizational culture features. The *involvement culture* is the most suitable to develop efficient informal communication. The *involvement culture* is internally oriented and with a clear focus on the relationship between organizational members [43]. It focuses on the dynamics of internal integration, by developing affinity between members. Figure 1 shows Danison and Mishra's [43] scheme of organizational cultures.

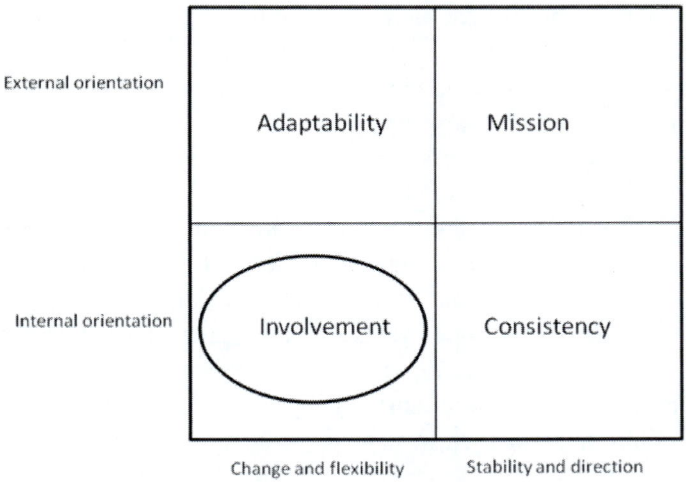

Source: Denison and Mishra, 1995.

Figure 1. Models of cultural traits.

Within healthcare organizations, the development of a pattern of shared values between professionals may contribute to the creation of an *involvement culture* on which a high quality communication and consequently high-qualified processes of care are based.

Values Congruence and Predictability

The value congruence affects *Predictability* of the organizational processes. Predictability represents a critical dimension within healthcare organizations, due to the high presence of interdependence between professionals, units and departments. Interdependence is the extent to which a person, a unit or an organization is dependent on others [44]. Three types of interdependencies have been studied: "Pooled interdependence," "Sequential interdependence," and "Reciprocal interdependence." Pooled interdependence concerns those organizational structures where each organizational department or business unit performs completely separate functions. In the pooled interdependence model, departments do not interact directly and they do not directly depend on each other. Each of them contributes with individual pieces to the same overall puzzle. Sequential Interdependence occurs when a unit produces the output required for the performance of the next. Finally with reciprocal interdependence the output of a unit (or department) becomes the input of another, following a cyclical approach. In this circumstance the intensity of interaction is at the highest level. Reciprocal models are the most complex and difficult to manage.

Managers can lead interdependencies by using various coordination mechanisms. For example, a pooled interdependency requires standardization in rules and operating procedures, while a sequential interdependency can be managed by using plans and schedules. Reciprocal interdependences are managed using information sharing and mutual adjustments.

Although healthcare organizations provide examples of all the three cited types, the reciprocal interdependences are the most diffused in contexts where the constant interaction between different specialties and units is strategic. For instance within the emergency care area, reciprocal interactions are the necessary condition to provide care.

By creating a common pattern of shared values, the level of predictability of activities and tasks increases, thus facilitating the reciprocal interdependence.

Values Congruence and Attraction – Selection - Attrition Model

The similarity between organizational members occurs thanks to the attraction- selection- attrition model [29]. This represents quite a spontaneous phenomenon able to create affinity in individuals belonging to the same organization. Value congruence represents a fundamental factor, by creating a uniform workplace. Although the attraction- selection- attrition model may generate a good level of communication and integration between group members, if not well managed it may cause an excess of homogeneity and cohesion. This negative consequence, named "*groupthink phenomenon,*" is the cause of not rational and useless solutions proposed by a vast number of groups. Within healthcare organizations, excessive group cohesion can be a threat for the success of healthcare processes. Although the values congruence is fundamental to guarantee a patient- oriented approach, healthcare managers need to maintain the groups' cohesion within physiological limits. Box 1 provides a description of the "*groupthink phenomenon,*" its causes and few recommendations for managers who want to prevent it.

Box 1. The groupthink phenomenon

According to Janis [30] groupthink can be defined as an excessive form of cohesion among the group members, whose need to be part of it is stronger than anything else. One of its main implications is the group members' willingness to reach unanimity quickly on any decision. In order to maintain a relaxed atmosphere group members suppress personal doubts following the prevailing opinion. Solutions result scarcely creative and qualitatively sub-optimal, compared with those reached individually, or by excessively close groups.

Managers can try to avoid the groupthink phenomenon intercepting a few warning signs indicated by Janis [30]:

- The overestimation of the group: it includes the illusion of invulnerability of the group members;
- A closed mindedness;
- The pressure towards uniformity by following self-censorship, a direct pressure on dissenters, the illusion of the unanimity, and self-appointed mind guards.

Other symptoms are the selection bias of the information and of alternatives. Excessively cohesive group members may fail to examine risks, to reconsider rejected alternatives, to select and process information.

The main recommendations provided by Janis [30] focus on the managers' active role in the groups' revitalization.

- Open climate. Each member should be a critical evaluator of actions and solutions proposed by the group. Criticism can be successful if managers encourage its giving and accepting.
- Impartiality. Leaders should be impartial and they must avoid showing personal preferences during the group discussion.
- Parallel work. Different groups and group leaders should face the same problem in parallel.

- Splitting. Group members must be divided into various sub-groups in order to assess the effectiveness and the quality of the solutions proposed.

- Open discussion. Each group member should privately discuss issues and solutions proposed in order to test reactions, and then report to the group.
- Devil's advocate. The introduction of one or more Devil's advocates during the meetings can revitalize the group decision-making processes.
- Extra time. In situation of conflicts, extra time should be devoted to interpret warning signals from rivals and to construct alternative scenarios of their intentions.
- Second chance. Before going public, it can be useful to reconsider the decisions in second chance meetings, in order to modify or improve the solutions proposed.

Box 2. Group revitalizing strategies

The Devil's advocacy and the dialectical inquiry are based on a stimulated conflict, able to reduce the excessive cohesion within the group [45].

The Devil's advocacy strategy improves the quality of group decisions, introducing stimulated conflict into the decision making process. It eliminates premature inhibitions and conformity of the group members. The main points are:

- Once the group has formulated the solutions of the problem assigned, those solutions are given to one (or more than one) member of the staff: the Devil's advocacy;
- Devil's advocacy has been instructed to find the weak point of the solutions;
- If the Devil's advocacy approves the solution, it means that it is free from groupthink effects and qualitatively good.
- It is useful to rotate the role of the Devil's advocacy in order to avoid conflicts and to help the development of good communication skills between the members of the organization.

The dialectical inquiry is a further approach to stimulate positive group conflicts. The technique is based on Plato dialectic school of philosophy approach. In ancient Greece the debates between Plato and his followers started from opposite positions: the thesis and the anti-thesis. By adopting this approach, group members progressively show opposite viewpoints, until they reach a univocal solution, arising from opposing sets of ideas. [46].

If it is not possible to avoid the groupthink phenomenon from occurring, literature provides two methods able to help group revitalization: the Devil's advocate and the dialectical inquiry. Box 2 provides the fundamental features of both strategies.

Due to the double effect of the Attraction, managers should pay attention to correctly balance work values congruence and rationality of the decision making processes.

Value Congruence and Trust

The last dimension analyzed by Edward and Cable [34] concerns the Trust of employees in the organization. Trust is defined as "*a leap of faith*" to which individuals are naturally disposed [47]. At an organizational level, trust implies the willingness of the employee to accept and observe the rules imposed by the organization. Although the willingness tends to decrease in correspondence with high professional autonomy, this is the case with physicians [42, 48], some conditions such as economic stability of the engagement, the major competencies recognized to the manager, and the trust in the mission and goals of the organization [42] help to increase it. In correspondence with a high level of trust in the mission and goals of the organization even physicians become more prone to collaborate with each other sharing information, opinions and goals.

Within organizations, it is possible to recognize two levels of trust (Figure 2). The first level concerns the relationship between colleagues, while the second concerns the trust reposed by the employees in the organization.

Interpersonal trust is able to create a positive organizational climate and a good level of integration between colleagues. Organizational trust allows the employees to believe in the organization's principles, thus accepting the authority and the limitation of their professional autonomy.

In general, the creation of a similar pattern of values among employees creates a good level of integration in the whole organization.

As we have observed in this section, the organizational dimensions of the communication, predictability, attraction and trust are positively modified by work values congruence. It in turn affects the level of organizational integration and the organizational outcomes (Figure 3).

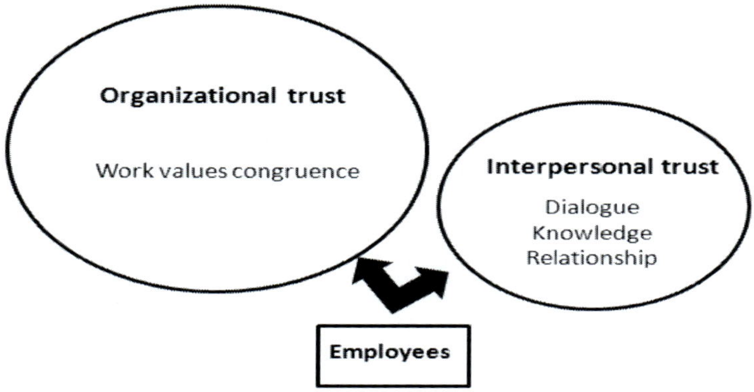

Figure 2. Levels of trust.

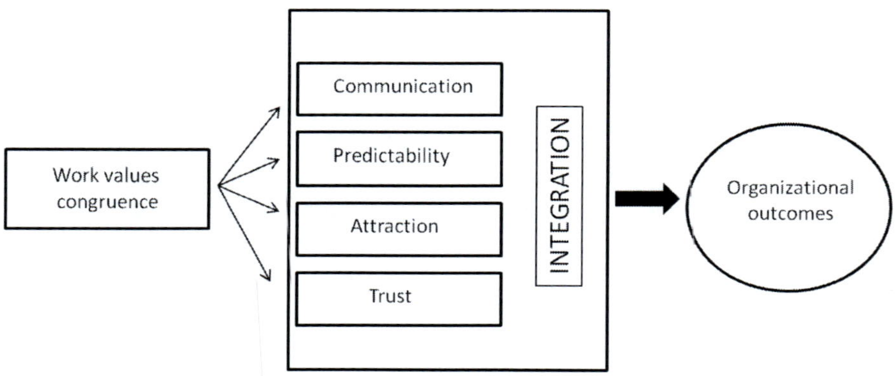

Adapted from Edwars and Carle, 2009

Figure 3. The role and influence of work values congruence on organizational outcomes.

Although the outcome measurement is quite easy in most organizations, within healthcare some significant issues make it difficult.

First, it is hard to consider the impact of healthcare procedures on patients, due to the difference between the concepts of output and outcomes. Moreover, in a more general perspective, the performance of healthcare organizations can be measured as the extent to which they provide healthcare services satisfying for both patients and employees. As we will explain in this chapter, employee satisfaction represents a fundamental condition to guarantee a real commitment of physicians and nurses on healthcare procedures. The commitment increases the work values alignment, which in turn affects employee satisfaction, creating a virtuous process as illustrated in Figure 4.

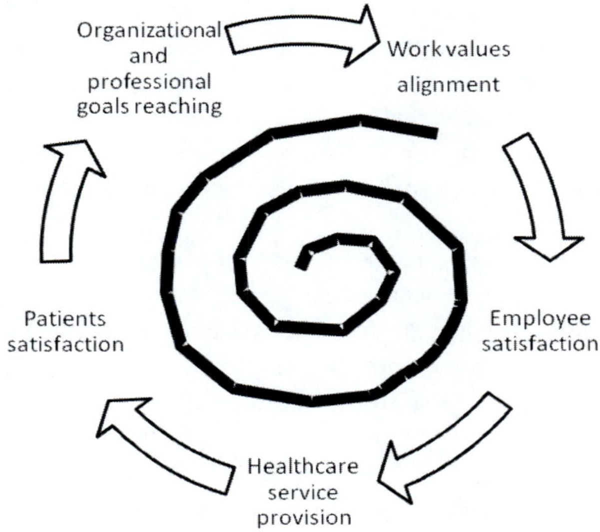

Figure 4. The virtuous cycle of values alignment.

PERFORMANCE MEASUREMENT WITHIN HEALTHCARE ORGANIZATIONS

A high performance healthcare organization is customer-oriented and focused on client satisfaction. Its first aim is to constantly improve the quality of products and services. High-performance systems are based on a work organization in which roles are designed and acted to achieve flexibility. High-performance systems ensure that workers are equipped with the knowledge and the skills required to reach positive goals. Going into detail, high performance systems promote group works and discussions, together with focusing on the improvement of relational and behavioral skills. They provide recruitment and selection policies able to attract and retain people characterized by strong motivation. Furthermore, a high performance organization implies guarantees of job security, equity in the internal careers, and the provision of frequent feedback to employees [49].

Through the above-mentioned tools, it is possible to create high committed organizations, thus establishing trusting relationships and encouraging and fostering changes [50]. By developing a climate of trust where innovation and risk-taking are encouraged and reasonably rewarded, decision makers provide real support to the performance of management. Moreover, the commitment of each organizational level and the employees' empowerment are necessary in this perspective [51]. While managers have the global vision of the organization and of its mission, employees have the tools and the skills to realize it. For that reason, it is necessary that responsibility, information and even the leadership are shared with all the members of the organization [52].

Within the healthcare context, besides the need to engage committed employees, performance management arises from important institutional changes. Traditionally the managerial systems were interested in the healthcare service provision, without taking into consideration the economic side. Due to the following reasons however, much attention has progressively been paid to the introduction of performance management systems [53].

- The growing demand for the health services, due to ageing and a widespread awareness about healthcare issues. The increasing level of patient knowledge jointly with their active involvement in decision-making processes affects the choice of the hospital. The success of healthcare organizations depends on the ability of both constantly improving their performances, and focusing their efforts on specific strategic priorities, responding punctually to stakeholders' expectations.
- The continuous technological development. In the next few years, ICT will play a vital role in the management of health care organizations. The growing relationship between users will become a real source of competitive advantage.
- Institutional attention on the quality of care provided by healthcare organizations. The ability of a healthcare organization to fulfill the expectations of external stakeholders is fundamental for its survival.

Besides the previously mentioned reasons, performance measurement in healthcare organizations is necessary for the employees' empowerment. Starting from the employee satisfaction and the organizational commitment of individuals it is possible to obtain highly-qualified care that in turn affects external expectations, thus creating the virtuous cycle showed in Figure 4.

The next paragraph analyzes the role played by employee satisfaction and its effect on work values alignment.

INDIVIDUAL AND ORGANIZATIONAL VALUES: THE ROLE OF JOB SATISFACTION

The central point of the present paragraph is the analysis of job satisfaction, in the attempt to understand how work values congruence can modify the individual orientation toward work. Literature affirms that job satisfaction represents the projection of the extent to which an individual is positively oriented toward his or her job [54]. As stated before, within healthcare organizations, job satisfaction assumes relevance by predicting several job-related behaviors, such as citizenship, turnover intentions, and performance of professionals [55, 56]. Satisfied physicians and nurses perform their activities with enthusiasm, thereby providing higher quality services to patients, who will be satisfied in turn. According to the previously cited statement, the positive employee predisposition and commitment are contingent upon the existing fit between organizational characteristics and personal traits of individuals [57].

Although both job satisfaction and organizational commitment can strongly contribute to the development of a positive organizational climate and good relationships, it is necessary to make a distinction between them. Organizational commitment is a personal involvement in the goals and mission of the organization. Job satisfaction instead represents a positive response to specific aspects of the work [58]. In correspondence to an adequate level of satisfaction, individuals develop an emotional response or an affective feeling towards work, which can have an impact on motivation, performance, but also a sense of belonging to the organization [47].

In the attempt to identify how individual satisfaction can be determined, Smith, Kendall e Hulin [59] developed the "Job Descriptive Index," by introducing in the evaluation four different dimensions: job, earning, career and quality of relationships. Job satisfaction is in fact closely related to the intrinsic features of work, but also to the extrinsic ones. Among the various causes however, three are the most important. The first one is equity. Organizational equity implies a constant benchmarking in terms of rewards and responsibilities that employees mutually exert in the workplace. In correspondence with low degrees of equity employees reveal less interest in contributing to organizational goals, showing a decrease in job satisfaction.

Furthermore, individual personal traits and genetic factors play a significant role in affecting the level of employee satisfaction.

In addition, literature has widely assumed that job satisfaction is closely related to the extent to which job characteristics meet employee needs. Satisfaction can be considered the correspondence between what a person expects from work and its actual fulfillment. If the expectations are higher than the real outcomes, the person will be disappointed until he/she gets closer results to his/her expectations. Managers can improve employee performance by designing a work environment, which appears to be coherent with the values, professed.

Furthermore, it is fundamental to analyze the consequences related to the presence/absence of job satisfaction. The presence implies motivation, corporate citizenship, job performance, whereas the absence denotes absenteeism, stress, intention to leave, turnover.

Among the cited consequences, the correlation between job satisfaction and performance is particularly interesting.

While on the one hand, it is possible to identify a positive correlation between these two dimensions, on the other their relationship is also influenced by environmental characteristics and individual differences. If managers want to increase the level of employee satisfaction, thus affecting performance, they carefully need to consider the role of the individual and organizational values alignment on employee satisfaction.

Within healthcare organizations, this role needs to be interpreted by taking into consideration the existence of different professional figures that may show unequal values. The next section is dedicated to the analysis of the attitudes of physicians and nurses toward work.

WORK VALUES AND PROFESSIONALISM: PHYSICIANS AND NURSES PERSPECTIVES

Healthcare professionals show heterogeneous attitudes toward work. Cicchetti [42], affirms that within healthcare organizations at least three different cultures coexist: physicians, nurses and administrative. We can easily assume that those cultural differences are responsible for heterogeneous predispositions and appreciation for what is important within the workplace. The dissimilarity can be linked to certain individual and professional traits, able to determine substantial differences in work values appreciation. For that reason, the present section analyzes physician and nurse determinants and consequences of the work values appreciation and congruence.

Starting from the analysis of physician determinants of work values appreciation, scholars have identified two personal and one professional feature, which can affect what is consider important in the work context.

The first personal feature is gender. Men doctors and women doctors show a different appreciation of work values [3, 20, 21], due to the *gender-specific socialization* [60-61]. Men seem to appreciate extrinsic work values such as career, power, and salary, while women show a greater interest in intrinsic and social values as for example the care of others or the ability to devote time to the family [62, 20]. Thanks to the "feminization of medicine" [65] the healthcare industry has progressively become one of the areas where gender diversity needs to be taken into consideration. Numerous studies reported a substantial increase in the number of women staffed in medical roles [63-64], thus implying relational and managerial changes. Compared to male doctors, female doctors are more interested in following a multidisciplinary approach during the process of care [65]. Moreover female doctors show higher levels of productivity compared to men, because of the need to balance work duties with family needs [63]. Gender differences are also linked to the access to leadership positions [66]. Apparently, many female doctors autonomously decide not to apply for leadership positions in their organizations because they do not feel suitable, or because of the difficulties to perform daily work activities with male colleagues [65]. Another significant personal trait that has been considered by literature is age. Generational differences in the work context can generate conflicts. Frequently, individuals belonging to different generations attribute various meanings to their work and perform different career choices [10, 1]. By adopting one of the most widely used classifications [67], it is possible to identify three different generations of professionals. The "Baby Boomer Generation" that includes subjects older than 46 years of age. "Generation X," is composed by individuals aged between 36 and 45 years; finally people younger than 36 years of age who are called the "Generation Y."

Within the healthcare organizations the risk of incurring in generational conflicts is extremely high due to the coexistence of different generations who interpret work in different ways [68-69]. For instance, doctors belonging to the Baby Boomer generation are totally committed to their profession, to the point that they mainly define themselves as "doctors." On the contrary, younger physicians are more interested in the work-life balance, thus considering the status of doctor less relevant [63].

Finally, the medical specialization is the last cause of the differences on a physician's work values appreciation. Literature shows that individuals with different specializations interpret in a heterogeneous manner the role of “doctor” [70-72]. Moreover, although a significant part of literature affirms that specialty choice by medical students is related to their personality traits [70], further evidence proves that the choice is also based on career and value aspirations [73]. Medical specialties can be classified into two main categories: *person-oriented* and *technique-oriented* specializations [74]. The *person-oriented* specialization includes family physicians, pediatricians, gynecologists and obstetricians, psychiatrists, and specialists in physical medicine. They show a holistic view of the patient and the relational component is at the base of the care process. In contrast, the *technique-oriented* physicians focus on technical skills, tools, and technologies that are useful for the healthcare service provision [70]. They are anesthesiologists, dermatologists, radiologists, emergency physicians, and pathologists. In terms of work values, technique-oriented specialists develop a deep interest in status and prestige [75] due to the very long and complex training courses they attend. On the contrary, doctors belonging to person-oriented specialties consider the social side of the work and the value of "self-direction" as two essential parts of their work. [72, 76].

While studies about a physician's work values focus on the effects of their individual and professional traits on work values appreciation, the panorama of studies on nurses’ work values focus on the effect that work values exert on their employee satisfaction, intention to leave and burn out. Furthermore, a part of literature shows that the issue of individual and organizational values alignment is an open question for nurses. For instance, scholars show that the environment in which nurses are employed and their personal attributes influence job satisfaction [77, 15, 78]. If not satisfied nurses may show high levels of stress, burn-out, mental and physical exhaustion [79], which can exert a negative effect on the care of patients. Although there are many reasons that can determine job dissatisfaction, (workloads or stress), a large part of literature recognizes that the value sharing between person and job context is an important predictor of job satisfaction [7, 15, 22].

Hegney and colleagues [15] provide an interesting example in this sense. By addressing a 16 item questionnaire to a significant number of nurses belonging to the Queensland Nurse Union, authors found that the workforce was in crisis regarding the value sharing with their organizations. It was due to a lack of alignment between what is important for nurses and what organization can assure them, thus affecting both nurse job satisfaction and their retention rate.

Takase and colleagues [80] provide a further interesting contribution on how work values affect the organizational behavior of nurses. By analyzing a sample of 319 Japanese nurses, they found a strict correlation between work values alignment and turnover intention. They show that when clinical challenges are higher or lower than what nurses expected, the intention to leave increases due to stress or atrophy.

Leiter and colleagues [81] deal with the problem of work values congruence in nurses. They begin the research analyzing the generational differences, and with the aim to provide an explanation of the burnout problem. According to Maslach and colleagues [82], the burnout results from chronic mismatches in important areas of work life, such as values. Congruence determines efforts and commitment in decision-making processes and when it fails, employees become susceptible of burnout [83, 81]. Furthermore, Leiter and colleagues [81] found that Generation X members consider work life less coherent with their personal values, generating a frustration feeling. In general, due to their negative evaluation of values congruence, Generation X nurses feel less compatible with their workplace, showing a higher rate of burnout with respect to Baby Boomers generation nurses.

Evidence coming from both professional profiles highlights the significant role that work values exert on attitudes and behaviors toward work, together with the job satisfaction (or dissatisfaction) affected by the fitting/not fitting between individuals and organizations. The following paragraphs confirm the above-cited assertions providing empirical evidence coming from a large sample of physicians and nurses staffed in 28 Italian hospitals.

EMPIRICAL ANALYSIS: PROFESSIONAL DIFFERENCES IN THE WORK VALUES GRADING

In order to investigate the effects of work values congruence on employee satisfaction, we performed an empirical analysis. We used data about individual work values preferences exhibited by healthcare professionals staffed in 44 clinical directorates[3], belonging to 28 Italian hospitals. Individual, demographic and gender differences affect the health professional's propensities, attitudes, and behaviors in the workplace [84, 85, 75]. They are responsible for variations in terms of job satisfaction [38, 29, 37, 22].

Data and Methods

Participants

Our sample consists of 596 doctors and 2001 nurses, who are mainly women (70.2%). The largest age group of respondents included individuals aged 46–50 years (21.7%), followed by physicians and nurses aged 41–45 years (20.6%). The majority of respondents were staffed in complex ward units (71%) and their average length of service was 13.8 years.

Procedures and Instruments

Data were collected as part of a broad research project about the clinical directorate model. Anonymous behavioral questionnaires were administered to physicians and nurses staffed in 44 clinical directorates [88-90] belonging to 28 healthcare organizations. Behavioral surveys were preceded by a meeting with the department Director and with representatives of the Department Assembly, in order to explain the objectives of the survey and to provide instructions on how to fill out the questionnaire. A letter of request for cooperation with the research accompanied the questionnaire. Each department was responsible for the preparation, distribution, and collection of completed questionnaires. In order to ensure anonymity, a box to collect the completed questionnaires was available in each department.

The questionnaire was composed of three sections that collected the following data: (1) general employee characteristics (e.g., gender, age, and tenure), (2) physician satisfaction before and after the introduction of the departmental model, (3) work values grading.

In order to assess how work values congruence determines an increase in job satisfaction, we used two levels of questions. The first level concerns the overall job satisfaction of individuals, while the second one assessed the extent to which employee satisfaction was modified after the introduction of the clinical directorate model. We decided to test the increase of employee satisfaction after the introduction of this new organizational arrangement

[3] For more details about clinical directorate model see [86-88].

because it better forms the concept of the working group. The similarity between clinical directorates and divisional units allows physicians and nurses to properly measure the work value congruence with their working group. A 4-point Likert scale was used to rate questionnaire answers: 1 = strongly disagree to 4 = strongly agree.

Concerning the work values grading section Hofstede [91] proposed to consider the level of importance attributed by employees to the main features characterizing their ideal working environment [21]. Therefore, the grading of work values was performed by asking the respondents to rank 10 work values from 1 to 10, with "1" indicating the most important and "10" indicating marginal importance. The work values mentioned in the questionnaire included earning, exploitation of results, career, climate, acknowledgement of skills, workload, availability of information, training, decision making, and freedom of initiative. Within the questionnaire each value was preceded by the statement: "*In my work, it would be important that...*" [70].

Finally, we gathered data on the institutional profile of each participating hospital and the internal features of each clinical directorate through a survey conducted by the Italian Ministry of Health during the same period.

Variables

Overall Job Satisfaction Improvement

It measures the increase of employee self-reported overall job satisfaction after the introduction of the clinical directorate. We used two levels of questions: "I'm satisfied working for this organization," and: "As a result of the introduction of the clinical directorate, my satisfaction has improved." Both sentences were assessed using a four-point Likert scale. When the difference between the two statements was positive we hypothesize an improvement in job satisfaction. In this circumstance, we attributed value 1, otherwise we assigned the value 0.

Work Values Congruence

For the purpose of this chapter, we used 9 of the 10 ranked work values. We grouped the 9 values into four main categories: intrinsic, extrinsic, social, and status-related work values. The variable "Extrinsic Work Values" has been calculated as the mean degree of importance attributed to the values: *Earnings* and *Career*. The variable "Intrinsic Work Values" is instead the mean of the degree of importance attributed to the values: *Exploitation of Results*, *Acknowledgement of Skills*, *Training*, and *Freedom of Initiative*. The "Status-related Work Values" variable has been calculated as the mean degree of importance attributed to the value: *Decision Making*. Finally the variable "Social-related work Values" concerns the mean degree of importance attributed to the values: *Climate* and *Workload*. In order to analyze the congruence between the individual and organizational values, we compared the individual work values grading to the general grading declared by other colleagues staffed in the same clinical directorate. When there was congruence we assigned value 1, otherwise we assigned value 0.

Institutional Profiles

Hospitals in Italy are classified into four main institutional categories: Hospital Trusts, LHU's Hospitals, Teaching Hospitals, and Research Hospitals[4]. In this chapter we employed 4 dummy variables, one for each category of hospitals.

Clinical Directorates Criteria

The set of 3 dummy variables, used to identify each category of clinical directorate, captures the different criteria according to which clinical wards were grouped together into newly formed directorates. Those criteria were labeled "Process-Integration," "Specialty-Integration," and "Mixed-Integration." "Process- Integration" was used as a baseline in the regression model.

Belonging

This dichotomous variable had a value of "1" if the surveyed employees belonged to a simple operating unit, or a value of "0" if he/she belonged to a complex unit.

Gender

This variable was also scored as a dichotomous value, with "1" indicating female gender and "0" indicating male gender.

Age

Respondents were classified into six categories by age, with each category corresponding to a dichotomous variable, as follows: up to 36 years old; 36-40

[4] For more details about institutional profiles of hospitals, please see chapter one.

years old; 41-45; 46-50; 51-55; older than 56. The latter class was identified as the base line.

Organizational Tenure

This continuous variable (min = 0, max = 42) indicated the length of service of the respondents in years.

Job Role

A value of "1" was assigned to physicians and "0" value to the remaining healthcare professions.

Analysis and Results

In this chapter, we performed two levels of analysis. The first level focuses on the analysis of whether and under what conditions the work values congruence affects the increase in job satisfaction. We conducted an empirical analysis using the Ordered Logit regression model [92, 93]. The "overall job satisfaction improvement" represents the dependent variable of the first model on which we tested the effect of the different categories of work values. Control variables have also been employed. Table 1 shows the results of the first level of analysis.

The results of Table 1 show a positive and significant probability that the overall job satisfaction improvement is affected by the extrinsic work values congruence ($\beta = 0.516$, $p \leq 0.05$). Even the intrinsic work values congruence ($\beta = 0.349$, $p \leq 0.01$) increases the probability to observe an increase in job satisfaction. On the contrary, the congruence on the status related work values and the congruence on the social work values do not exert any significant impact on the "overall job satisfaction improvement." The probability that the overall job satisfaction improves after the introduction of the clinical directorate, increases for physicians and nurses belonging to a simple ward unit ($\beta = 0.426$, $p \leq 0.01$). Finally, physicians show a positive and significant probability of improvement in overall job satisfaction with respect to nurses ($\beta = 0.380$, $p \leq 0.\ 1$).

Table 1. Results of Ordered Logistic Regression (first level of analysis)

Overall Job satisfaction improvement	
Extrinsic work values congruence	0.516*
	(0.242)
Intrinsic work values congruence	0.349**
	(0.142)
Status related work values congruence	0.195
	(0.205)
Social work values congruence	-0.296
	(0.524)
Trust Hospitals	-0.067
	(0.402)
LHU's Hospitals	-0.042
	(0.303)
Teaching Hospitals	0.094
	(0.298)
Specialty directorates	0.325
	(0.215)
Mixed directorates	-0.726
	(0.715)
Simple ward unit belonging=1	0.426**
	(0.162)
Women=1	-0.288
	(0.232)
Organizational tenure	-0.001
	(0.013)
Up to 36 years	0.287
	(0.432)
36-40 years	0.088
	(0.473)
41-45 years	0.160
	(0.381)
46-50 years	0.051
	(0.415)
51-55 years	0.271
	(0.322)
Job role, physician= 1	0.380●
	(0.218)
Constant	-2.84
	(0.501)
Log Pseudo Likelihood	-603.02714
Wald Chi2	47.86
prob> chi2	0.0002
Pseudo R2	0.0228
Number of observations	2597

●$p \leq 0.1$; *$p \leq 0.05$; **$p \leq 0.01$; ***$p \leq 0.001$.

Table 2. Results of Ordered Logistic Regression (second level of analysis)

	Model I extrinsic work values congruence	*Model II Intrinsic work values congruence*	*Model III Status work values congruence*	*Model IV Social work values congruence*
Job role, physician= 1	-0.272	0.165	0.221●	0.066
	(0.171)	(0.338)	(0.121)	(0.488)
Women=1	0.138	-0.035	0.098	0.399***
	(0.087)	(0.270)	(0.114)	(0.104)
Up to 36 years	-0.085	-1.618**	-0.141	-0.143
	(0.196)	(0.665)	(0.207)	(0.175)
36-40 years	-0.051	-0.518	-0.123	-0.330*
	(0.211)	(0.586)	(0.179)	(0.153)
41-45 years	0.126	-0.584	0.062	-0.191
	(0.143)	(0.496)	(0.161)	(0.137)
46-50 years	0.163	-1.257*	0.080	-0.226
	(0.139)	(0.574)	(0.155)	(0.165)
51-55 years	0.101	-1.101*	0.009	0.010
	(0.149)	(0.473)	(0.172)	(0.165)
Organizational tenure	0.012*	-0.021	-0.006	-0.006
	(0.005)	(0.022)	(0.007)	(0.005)
Simple ward unit belonging=1	-0.006	0.139	0.039	-0.146
	(0.110)	(0.315)	(0.114)	(0.078)
Process directorate	-0.057	0.724	0.292***	0.194*
	(0.347)	(0.713)	(0.079)	(0.097)
Specialty directorate	0.018	0.170	0.304***	0.179●
	(0.339)	(0.701)	(0.095)	(0.094)
Teaching Hospital	0.033	-0.027	-0.241	-0.090
	(0.298)	(0.377)	(0.252)	(0.170)
Trust Hospital	0.514	-0.383	0.008	-0.140
	(0.361)	(0.619)	(0.262)	(0.203)
LHU's Hospital	0.162	-0.183	-0.184	-0.079
	(0.316)	(0.429)	(0.265)	(0.184)
Constant	-0.482	-2.98**	-1.610***	-0.845***
	(0.431)	(1.008)	(0.342)	(0.212)
Log Pseudo Likelihood	-1771.9008	-289.96898	-1262.1708	-1619.1035
Wald Chi2	37.94	24.04	45.86	83.07
Prob> chi2	0.0005	0.0453	0.0000	0.0000
Pseudo R2	0.0154	0.0341	0.0045	0.0068
Number of observations	2597	2597	2597	2597

●$p \leq 0.1$; *$p \leq 0.05$; **$p \leq 0.01$; ***$p \leq 0.001$.

The aim of the second level of analysis is to test whether the individual, the professional or the organizational perspectives determine the congruence or the incongruence between the individual values and the organizational (departmental) ones. We performed four ordered logistic regressions. Each model presents as a dependent variable, one of the four work value categories (extrinsic, intrinsic, social related and status related). The professional role, gender, age, organizational tenure, belonging, institutional profile, and departmental aggregating criteria represent the independent variables. Table 2 shows the results of the second level of analysis.

The results in Table 2 show the existence of some interesting dimensions that are able to affect the probability to find work values congruence within clinical directorates. When considering the job role, physicians show a positive and significant probability to show status related work values congruence with respect to nurses ($\beta = 0.221$, $p \leq 0.1$). When considering gender, women show a positive and significant probability to display social work values congruence in compared to men ($\beta = 0.399$, $p \leq 0.001$). Even the dimension of age exerts an effect on work values congruence. Going into details, the youngest age classes (<36 years old, 46-50 and 51-55) show negative coefficients concerning the probability to find congruence on intrinsic work values compared to the oldest age group of professionals ($\beta = -1.618$, $p \leq 0.01$). Compared to the same class, the 36-40 aged employees show a negative coefficient when considering the probability to find a social work values congruence ($\beta = -0.330$, $p \leq 0.05$). The organizational tenure positively affects the probability to find the extrinsic work values congruence ($\beta = 0.012$, $p \leq 0.05$). Finally, the criteria used to design clinical directorates exert an impact on the probability to find a work values congruence. For example, the probability to find the status work values congruence is positively affected by both conditions of being staffed within process directorates ($\beta = 0.292$, $p \leq 0.00$) and specialty directorates ($\beta = 0.304$, $p \leq 0.001$). Even social work values congruence is affected by the aggregating criteria of clinical directorates, both process directorates ($\beta = 0.194$, $p \leq 0.05$), and specialty ones ($\beta = 0.179$, $p \leq 0.1$).

DO INDIVIDUALS SHAPE ORGANIZATIONS? THE EFFECT ON JOB SATISFACTION

The aim of this chapter is to explore whether work values congruence within healthcare organizations positively affects physicians and nurses' satisfaction. Starting from the individual preferences about work values and thus comparing those preferences with the workplace values, it has been possible to determine the work values congruence or incongruence. Demographic, gender, and professional characteristics were examined, as well as a few characteristics of the organizational context in which doctors and nurses work. A second level of analysis employed those characteristics to determine their effect on the probability to observe the congruence between individual and organizational values.

The first level of analysis shows that both extrinsic and intrinsic work values positively affect the improvement of employee satisfaction. Results show that in correspondence with the congruence between individual and organizational intrinsic values (learning opportunities, autonomy, responsibility, and creativity), the level of employee satisfaction increases. The same happens when the organization is able to fill the individual expectation concerning extrinsic work values such as salary or career advancements. On the contrary, the congruence between individual and organizational status-related work values and social-related work values does not affect the employee satisfaction improvement. Although the congruence in social work values and status work value may satisfy the highest level of the Maslow's hierarchy in terms of self- actualization (status related values), or social identity (social related values), it does not exert a direct effect on job satisfaction improvement.

A few control variables help us to better understand when an improvement of employee satisfaction occurs. As illustrated in Table 1, within simple ward units the probability to observe an increase in job satisfaction is higher than in complex ward units. It may be related to both the better relationship between colleagues and the lower degree of workloads, emerging in simple organizational contexts.

Finally, the work role exerts an impact on job satisfaction increase. Physicians were more satisfied than nurses regarding the introduction of clinical directorates. Although considering the individual openness to experiences as an explanation of why some people are more prone to accept changes than others [89], a possible interpretation of the results is that the workload of nurses has become extremely heavy following the introduction of the new organizational model [94].

By considering the second level of analysis we found that status work value congruence has been achieved by physicians but not by nurses. Physicians have more career advancement probabilities than nurses and are more involved into the decision making processes [86]. For these reasons they find better fulfillment of their status expectations.

Even individual characteristics as gender and age play an important role in the work values congruence realization. Men show greater appreciation for extrinsic work values such as career, power, and earning, whereas women show a greater appreciation for intrinsic and social work values [62, 20]. For that reason women's effort is oriented to contribute to the development of a workplace characterized by those values connected with the relational component of the job, such as organizational climate, altruistic behavior, and care of colleagues [6, 18].

When considering age, results indicate that different generations show different probabilities to find coherence within the workplace for heterogeneous categories of values. It is mainly due to the heterogeneous conceptions of work, as well as differences in life and family experiences [18].

In correspondence with the increase of organizational tenure the probability to find coherence between individual and organizational extrinsic work values increases, thanks to the expected income progression within organizations.

Results demonstrate that the criteria used to design clinical directorates affect the probability to establish congruence between individual and organizational status and social related work values, especially within specialty oriented and process oriented directorates. It means that when the designing criteria are clear [88; 89] the decision making involvement and the quality of the relationships with colleagues and chiefs increase.

The results achieved in this chapter have several managerial and policy implications. From a managerial point-of-view, the knowledge of employees' work values is essential to determine how to optimize work in health care organizations. Furthermore, it is essential to provide to each person the value that he/she needs in order to achieve a good level of satisfaction within the organizational context. Ideally, the hospital should firstly determine the work values of the individuals and then it should schedule the work in order to satisfy people. From the point-of-view of policymaking, it is important to clarify with aspiring doctors and nurses what values they may potentially develop and satisfy through their career. Moreover, it is important that health managers recognize and appreciate the diversity of values and abilities of different types of clinical directorate structures to meet their expectations.

CONCLUSION

Within this chapter we provide a significant contribution to the debate on the key role of work values within healthcare organizations. In addition we offer some reflections about the importance of achieving a right amount of congruence between the individual and the organizational values pattern. Due to the effect of work values congruence on integration, we have underlined how managers can improve the communication between colleagues, by creating a work context in which each professional is able to fulfill his/her expectations. Moreover, it was explained how managers should avoid the groupthink phenomenon that drives to an excessive congruence, generating negative effects in terms of group performance.

We proved empirically that work values congruence affects job satisfaction by performing a regression analysis. Results show that the individual and organizational work values congruence in terms of extrinsic and intrinsic values is able to determine an improvement in job satisfaction, whereas the same effect is not recognizable for the congruence in terms of social and status related values. A second level of analysis has been performed in order to show which features allow the congruence among the different categories of work values. Professional role, gender and age affect this probability, as well some organizational features.

REFERENCES

[1] Twenge, Jean M., Stacy M. Campbell, Brian J. Hoffman, and Charles E. Lance. 2010. "Generational differences in work values: leisure and extrinsic values increasing, social and intrinsic values decreasing." *Journal of Management*, 36 (5): 1117-1142.

[2] Super, Donald E. 1970. *Manual: Work values inventory*, Houghton-Miffin, Boston.

[3] Li, Wanxian, Xinmei Liu and Weiwu Wan. 2008. "Demographic effect of work values and their management implications." *Journal of Business Etichs*, 81: 875-885.

[4] Dose, Jennifer J. 1997. "Work values and the integrative frame work and illustrative application to organizational socialization." *Journal of Occupational and Organizational Psychology*, 70: 219-241.

[5] Ros, Maria, Shalom H. Schwartz, and Shoshana Surkiss. 1999. "Basic individual values, work values and the meaning of the work." *Applied Psychology: an international review*, 48: 49-71.

[6] Jin, Jing and James Rounds. 2012. "Stability and change in work values: a meta- analysis of longitudinal studies." *Journal of Vocational Behavior*, 80: 326-339.

[7] Taris, Ruben and Jan A. Feji. 2001. "Longitudinal examination of the relationship between supplies –values fit and work outcomes." *Applied Psychology: an international review*, 50: 52-80.

[8] Hansen, Jo-Ida C., and Melanie E. Leuty. 2012. "Work values across generations." *Journal of Career Assessment*, 20(1): 34-52.

[9] Shapira, Zur and Terry L. Griffith. 1990. "Comparing work values of engineers with managers, production and clerical workers: a multivariate analysis." *Journal of Organizational Behavior*, 11 (4): 281-292.

[10] Gursoy, Dogan, Thomas A. Maier, and Christina Chi G. 2008. "Generational differences: An examination of work values and generational gaps in the hospitality workforce." *International Journal of Hospitality Management*, 27: 448-458.

[11] Kirkpatrick Johnson, Monica, Rayana A. Sage, and Jeylan T. Mortimer. 2012. "Work Values, Early Career Difficulties, and the U.S. Economic Recession." *Social Psychology Quarterly*, 75(3): 242-267.

[12] Deci, Edward and Richard M. Ryan. 1985. *Intrinsic motivation and self-determination in human behavior*. New York: Plenum.

[13] Porter, Lyman W., and Edward E. Lawler. 1968. *Managerial attitudes and performance*. Homewood, IL: Dorsey Press.

[14] Ryan, Richard M., and Edward Deci. 2000. "Self- determination theory and the facilitation of intrinsic motivation, social development and well-being." *American Psychologist*, 55: 68-78.

[15] Hegney, Desley, Ashley Plank and Victoria Parker. 2006. "Extrinsic and intrinsic work values: their impact on job satisfaction in nursing." *Journal of nursing management*, 14: 271-281.

[16] Schwartz, Shalom H. 1992. "Universal in the content and structure of values: theoretical advances and empirical tests in 20 countries." In *Advances in experimental psychology* edited by Mark P. Zanna, and Mark P. Zanna, Academic Press, San Diego, CA, 25: 1-65.

[17] Herzberg, Frederick. 1987. "One more time: how do you motivate employees?" *Harvard Business review*, 65 (5): 109-120.

[18] Cennamo, Lucy and Dianne Gardner. 2008. "Generational differences in work values, outcomes and person- organization values fit." *Journal of Managerial Psychology*, 23 (8): 891-906.

[19] Parry, Emma and Peter Urwin. 2011. "Generational differences in work values: a review theory and evidence." *International Journal of Management Reviews*, 13: 79-96.

[20] Hirschi, Andreas and Sebastian Fischer. 2013. "Work values as predictors of entrepreneurial career intentions." *Career Development International*, 18, 3: 216-231.

[21] Berings, Dries and Stef Adriaenssens. 2012. "The role of business ethics, personality, work values and gender in vocational interest from adolescents." *Journal of Business ethics*, 106: 325-335.

[22] Ren, Ting. 2013. "Sectoral differences in value congruence and job attitudes: the case of nursing home employees." *Journal of business ethics*, 112: 213-224.

[23] Krau, Edgar. 1989. "The transition in life domain salience and the modification of work values between high school and adult employment." *Journal of vocational behavior*, 34: 100-116.

[24] Kirkpatrick Jonhson, Monica. 2005. "Family Roles and Work Values: Processes of Selection and Change." *Journal of Marriage and Family*, 67:113-138.

[25] Mortimer, Jeylan T., and Jon Lorence. 1979. "Work experience and occupational value socialization: a longitudinal study." *American journal of sociology*, 84: 1361-1385.

[26] Kirkpatrick Johnson, Monica. 2001. "Change in job values during the transition to adulthood." *Work and occupations*, 28: 315-345.

[27] Daehlen, Marianne. 2008. "Job satisfaction and job values among beginning nurses: a questionnaire survey." *International journal of nursing studies*, 45: 1789-1799.

[28] McAdams, Dan P., and Bradley D. Olson. 2010. "Personality Development: Continuity and Change Over the Life Course." *Annual review of psychology*, 61.

[29] Schneider, Benjamin. 1987. "The people make a place" *Personnel psychology*, 40: 437:453.

[30] Janis, Irving L. 1982. *Groupthink. A psychological study of policy decisions and flascoes*. Boston, Houghton Miffin Company.

[31] Cascio, Wayne F. 1999. *Costing human resources: the financial impact of behavior in organizations* (4th edition). Cincinnati, OH. South western.

[32] Riketta, Michael. 2005. Organizational identification: a meta- analysis. *Journal of vocational behavior*, 66: 358-384.

[33] Chatman, Jennifer A., 1989. Improving interactional organizational research: a model of person- organization fit. *Academy of management review*, 14: 333-349.

[34] Edwards, Jeffrey R., and Daniel M. Cable. 2009. "The Value of Value Congruence." *Journal of Applied Psychology*. 94(3): 654-677.

[35] Chatman, Jennifer A. 1991. "Matching people and organizations: selection and socialization in public accounting firms." *Administrative science quarterly*, 36: 459-484.

[36] Finegan, Joan E. 2000. "The impact of person and organizational value on organizational commitment." *Journal of Occupational and Organizational Psychology*, 73:149-169.

[37] Kristof-Brown, Amy L., Ryan D. Zimmerman, and Erin C. Johnson. 2005. "Consequences of individuals' fit at work: A meta-analysis of person-job, person-organization, person-group, and person-supervisor fit." *Personnel Psychology* 58: 281-342.

[38] O'Reilly, Charles A. and Chatman. 1986. Organizational commitment and psychological attachment: the effects of compliance, identification and internalization on prosocial behavior. *Journal of applied psychology*, 71 (3): 492-499.

[39] O'Reilly, Charles A., Jennifer Chatman, and David F. Caldwell. 1991. "People and organizational culture: a profile comparison approach to assessing person- organization fit." *Academy of management journal*, 34(3): 487-516.

[40] Meyer, Roger C., James H. Davis, and David F. Schoorman. 1995. An integrative model of organizational trust. *Academy of management review*, 20: 709-734.

[41] Daft, Richard. L. 2013. *Organizzazione Aziendale*. Apogeo (in Italian).

[42] Cicchetti, Americo. 2004. *La progettazione organizzativa*. Franco Angeli, Milano. (In Italian).

[43] Danison, Daniel R., and Aneil K. Mishra. 1995. "Toward a theory of organizational culture and effectiveness." *Organization science*, 6 (2): 204-223.

[44] Thompson, James D., 1967. *Organization in action*. McGraw Hill, New York.

[45] Lunenburg, Fred C. 2012. "Devil's advocacy and dialectical inquiry: antidotes to groupthink." *International journal of scholarly academic intellectual diversity*, 14 (1).

[46] Schweiger, David M., William R. Sandburg, and James W. Ragan. 1986. "Group approaches for improving strategic decision making: a comparative analysis of dialectical inquiry, devil's advocacy and consensus." *Academy of management journal*, 29: 149-159.

[47] Kreitner, Robert, and Angelo Kinicki A., 2013. *Organizational Behavior*. McGraw-Hill Higher Education.

[48] Freidson Eliot. 1970. "Profession of medicine: a study of the sociology of applied knowledge." *JAMA*, 214 (2): 376.

[49] Price Ilfryn. 2004. "Business critical FM." *Facilities*, 22 (13-14): 353-358.

[50] Pfeffer Jeffrey. 1998. *The human equation: building profits by putting people first*. Boston: Harward Business School press.

[51] Costa Giovanni and Martina Gianecchini. 2003. *Risorse umane, persone, relazioni, valori*. Mc Graw Hill. (In Italian).

[52] Murrell Kenneth L. and Mimi Meredith. 2000. *Empowering Employees*. Mc Graw Hill professional.

[53] Chow, Chee W., Denise Ganulin, Kamal Haddad, and Jim Williamson. 1998. "The balanced scorecard: a potent tool for energizing and focusing healthcare organizations." *Journal of healthcare management*. 43 (3).

[54] Cramer, Duncan 1996. "Job satisfaction and organizational continuance commitment: a two-wave panel study." *Journal of Organizational Behavior*, 17:389–400.

[55] Locke, Edwin A. 1976. "The nature and causes of job satisfaction." In *Handbook of industrial and organizational psychology*. edited by Dunnette MD, Chicago: Rand McNally: 1297–349.

[56] Kinicki, Angelo J., Frances M. McKee-Ryan, Chester A. Schriesheim, and Kenneth P. Carson. 2002. "Assessing the construct validity of the job descriptive index: a review and meta-analysis." *Journal of Applied Psychology*, 87: 14–32.

[57] Caldwell, Steven D., David Herold, and Donald B. Fedor. 2004. "Towards an understanding of the relationships between organizational change, individual differences, and changes in person-environment fit: a cross-level study." *Journal of Applied Psychology*, 89: 868–82.

[58] Williams, Larry J., and John T. Hazer J.T. 1986. "Antecedents and consequences of satisfaction and commitment in turnover models: a re-

analysis using latent variable structural equation methods." *Journal of applied psychology*, 72 (1): 219-231.

[59] Smith, Patricia C., Lorne M. Kendall and Charles L. Hulin. 1969. *The measurement of satisfaction in work and retirement*. Chicago: Rand Mc Nally.

[60] Halaby Charles N. 2003. "Where job values come from: family and schooling background, cognitive, ability and gender." *American Sociological Review*, 68 (2): 251-278.

[61] Rohan Meg. 2000. "A rose by any name? The values construct." *Personality and Social Psychology Review*, 4 (3): 255-277.

[62] Konrad Alison M., J.E. jr Ritchie, Pamela Lieb and Elizabeth Corrigal. 2000. "Sex differences and similarities in job attribute preferences: a meta-analysis." *Psychological Bulletin*, 26 (4): 593-641.

[63] Jovic, Emily, Jean E. Wallace, and Lane Lemaire. 2006. "The generation and gender shits in medicine: an exploratory survey of internal medicine physicians." *BMC Health Services Research*, 6(55): 1-10.

[64] Strong Erin A., Rochelle De Castro, Dana Sambuco, Abigail Stewart, Peter A. Ubel, Kent A. Griffith, and Reshma Jagsi. 2013. "Work–Life Balance in Academic Medicine: Narratives of Physician-Researchers and Their Mentors." *Journal of General Internal Medicine* 28(12):1596–603.

[65] Levinson, Wendy, and Nicole Lurie. 2004. "When Most are Women: What Lies Ahead?." *American College of Physicians*, 141: 471-474.

[66] Yedidia, Michael J., and Janet Bickel. 2001. "Why aren't there more women leaders in academic medicine? The views of clinical department chairs." *Academic Medicine*, 76:453–65.

[67] Lyons, Sean. 2004. "An exploration of generational values in life and at work," Ph.D. diss. Eric Sprott School of business, Carleton University, Ottawa Ontario.

[68] Dukerich, Janet M., Brian R. Golden, and Stephen M. Shortell. "Beauty is in the eye of the beholder: the impact of organizational identification, identity, and image on the cooperative behavior of physicians." *Administrative Science Quarterly*, 47: 507–533.

[69] Kreiner, Glen E., and Blake E. Ashforth. 2004. "Evidence toward an expanded model of organizational identification." *Journal of organizational behavior*, 25 (1): 1-27.

[70] Taber, Brian J., Paul J. Hartung, and Nicole J. Borges. 2011. "Personality and values as predictors of medical specialty choice." *Journal of Vocational Behavior*, 78: 202-209.

[71] Borges, Nicole J., and Denise D. Gibson. 2005. "Personality patterns of physicians in person- oriented and technique oriented specialties." *Journal of Vocational Behavior*, 67: 4-20.

[72] Bouwkamp-Memmer, Jennifer C., Susan C. Whiston, and Paul J. Hartung. 2013. "Work values and job satisfaction of family physicians." *Journal of Vocational Behavior*, 82: 248-255.

[73] Rogers, Mary E., and Judy Searle. 2009. "Factors influencing the practice choices of Australian medical students: a feasibility study." *The Australian Journal of Rural Health*, 17: 107-108.

[74] Yufit, Robert I., George H. Pollock, and Edward Wasserman. 1969. "Medical specialty choice and personality: initial results and predictions." *Archives of General Psychiatry*, 20: 80-99.

[75] Borges, Nicole J., and William R. Osmon. 2001. "Personality and medical specialty choice: technique orientation versus people orientation." *Journal of Vocational Behavior*, 58: 22-35.

[76] Eliason, Clair B., Clare E. Guse, and Mark S. Gottlieb. "Personal values of family physicians, practice satisfaction, and service to the underserved." *Archives of Family Medicine*, 9, 228–232.

[77] Wheeler, Hermann. 1997. Nurse occupational stress research, 3: a model of stress for research. *British journal of nursing*, 6 (16): 944-949.

[78] Adams, Ann E., and Senga Bond. 2000. "Hospital nurses' job satisfaction, individual and organizational characteristics." *Journal of advanced nursing*, 32: 536-543.

[79] Tummers, Glady E.R., Jan A. Landeweerd, and Godefridus G. van Merode. 2002. "Organization, work and work reactions: a study of the relationship between organizational aspects of nursing and nurses' work characteristics and work reactions." *Scandinavian journal of caring science*, 16: 52-58.

[80] Takase, Miyuki, Noriko Yamashitan and Keiko Oba. 2007. "Nurses' leaving intentions: antecedents and mediating factors." *Journal of advanced nursing*, 62(3): 295-306.

[81] Leiter, Michael P., Nicole J. Jackson, and Krystelle Shaughnessy. 2008. "Contrasting burnout, turnover intention, control, value congruence and knowledge sharing between Baby Boomers and Generation X." *Journal of nursing management*, 17: 100-109.

[82] Maslach, Christina, Wilmar B. Schaufeli, and Michael P. Leiter. 2001. "Job burnout." *Annual review of psychology*, 52: 397-422.

[83] Leiter, Michael P., and Christina Maslach. 2004. "Areas of worklife: a structured approach to organizational predictors of job burnout." *Emotional and psychological processes and positive intervention strategies research in occupational stress and well being*, 3: 91-134.

[84] Southard, Glenn and Jim Lewis. 2004. Building a workplace that Recognizes Generational Diversity. *Public Management.*

[85] Midttun Linda. 2007. Private or public? An empirical analysis of the importance of work values for work sector choice among Norwegian medical specialists. *Social Science and Medicine*, 64: 1265-1277.

[86] Lega, Federico. 2008. The Rise And Fall(Acy) of Clinical Directorates in Italy. *Health Policy*, 85: 252-262.

[87] Braithwaite, Jeffrey, Mary T. Westbrook, Don Hindle, Rick A. Iedema, and Daniel A. Black. 2006. "Does restructuring hospitals result in greater efficiency. An empirical test using diachronic data." *Health Services Management Research*, 19, 1-12.

[88] Mascia Daniele, Silvia Dello Russo, and Federica Morandi. 2015. "Exploring Professionals' Motivation to Lead: A Cross-level Study in the Healthcare Sector." *International Journal of Human Resource Management*, 26(12): 1622-1644.

[89] Mascia, Daniele, Federica Morandi and Americo Cicchetti. 2014. "Hospital restructuring and physicians job satisfaction: an empirical study." *Health Policy*, 114: 118-127.

[90] McNulty, Terry, and Edward Ferlie. 2004. "Process transformation: Limitations to radical organizational change within public service organizations." *Organization Studies*, 25: 1389-1412.

[91] Hofstede, Geert. 1980. *Culture's consequences: international differences in work related values*. Beverly Hills, CA: Sage.

[92] Long, J. Scott and Jeremy Freese. 2006. *Regression models for categorical depending variables using Stata. Second Edition*. Stata Press, College station Texas.

[93] Wooldridge, Jeffrey M. 2009. *Econometric Analysis of Cross Section and Panel Data*. Massachusetts Institute of Technology.

[94] Braithwaite, Jeffrey and Mary Westbrook. 2005. "Rethinking clinical organizational structures: an attitude survey of doctors, nurses and allied health staff in clinical directorates." *Journal of Health Service Research Policy*, 10(1): 10-17.

Chapter 5

The Strategy of Negotiating: Natural Predisposition and Organizational Needs

Abstract

Starting in the '90s in many countries physicians have progressively assumed managerial responsibilities within the workplace. The New Public Management (NPM) imposed entrepreneurial tasks on hospitals thus making it necessary to pay attention to both the quality and the operating costs of the healthcare service. Due to their new double role, physicians started to be involved in budgeting discussions, thus requiring them to play the role of negotiators. Moreover, this new double role has affected their ability to find a balance between administrative and clinical responsibilities, generating the need to negotiate internally.

The negotiation is a significant challenge to be explored, it being both externally and internally oriented. The external side of negotiation is essential to obtain advantages during the transactions, while the internal negotiation is strategic to interpret the new organizational roles correctly.

Thanks to a questionnaire-based survey, this chapter provides evidence about physicians' external and internal ability to negotiate and about their way to face managerial tasks.

Keywords: negotiation, role conflict, role ambiguity, negotiating traits

Introduction

The daily work activities of physicians require the ability to negotiate. Negotiation is a useful strategy to obtain a favorite position, without incurring in discussions and long and exhausting transactions. The general conception of the term negotiation indicates the attempt of an individual to obtain something from someone else, i.e., when sellers try to keep the price of a good unchanged and buyers want it reduced, until they reach (or not) an agreement. However, there is also an internally oriented view on negotiation. For example, career advancement may imply more money in exchange for less free time. In this circumstance, the employee needs to negotiate between two conflicting areas: freedom and prosperity.

Each of us negotiates continuously in daily life, but it is not common to be involved at the same time in both internal and external negotiations. However, it may happen in some circumstances. For instance, it is the case of physicians in managerial roles. In several countries, Italy among them, starting in the '90s, the New Public Management principles were introduced in different sectors. In the healthcare context, since the introduction of this innovation, physicians have been progressively involved in administrative tasks. One of the main consequences of the innovation was the physician's need to acquire negotiating abilities together with the need to find a balance between clinical and administrative activities.

Literature provides significant evidence on the physician's involvement in external and internal negotiating processes. However, the contributions to the topic are focused on the description of the processes of budgeting or on the assumption of administrative roles, without surveying physicians' opinions on it.

In the attempt to fill this gap, this chapter examines the current debate on the double side of negotiation together with providing an empirical exploration of this phenomenon. The main individual traits that emerged during the negotiating processes were analyzed together with the physicians' perception of both role conflict and role ambiguity coming from the assumption of new managerial roles.

Negotiation: Is It an Art or a Strategy?

Commonly, negotiation indicates the interaction between different entities united by the purpose of achieving mutual objectives.

During everyday life, and within organizations, negotiating processes, exchanges or transactions take place in order to obtain specific results and to preserve personal interests. Those interests may be public or private and they have the primary intent of satisfying in a reciprocal way, the parties actively involved in the negotiation.

The main reason, for which the negotiation processes happen, is that both the involved parties feel the necessity to pursue certain goals, which may change depending on the type of negotiation.

An assertive communication, diplomatic and responsible, can help to identify what the negotiating counterpart is trying to obtain, thus creating an alignment in terms of interests.

The relationship between the negotiator and his/her partner characterizes each negotiation. It is essential to find an assertive, proactive and consistent communication system between the two parties, which must be helpful in order to identify the actual objectives of the interlocutor. The negotiating process participants must be able to understand any emotional, psychological and managerial facet of the process.

In order to be effective, the negotiating processes need to be based on good communication. They must ensure individual, organizational, and social values creation for the two parties involved.

The “value added" can be considered as the achievement of a result that generates satisfaction and in turn represents the leitmotiv for the negotiating process excellence.

NEGOTIATION SKILLS AND STRATEGIES

A Brief Description of the “Good Negotiator”

The “good negotiator” can be identified through his/her communicative/relational competences together with his/her ability to know the interlocutor. The negotiator’s skills are extremely important since they affect the results of the transaction process. Due to the individual's disposition, personality, and the experiences characterizing the individual's life, each person is more or less able to negotiate. However, the features of the “good negotiator” can be gradually developed, thus becoming a new skill for the individual, which can exert an impact on his/her negotiating process.

The negotiator is an interpersonal communication facilitator, whose objective is to reach a safe and fair trade between the counterparts.

During the negotiation, it is useful to understand and to interpret each situation in order to prevent conflicts. The good negotiator is able to decode the counterpart's message and to communicate clearly the objectives, expectations and responsibilities of the transaction process.

Due to a lack of negotiating skills among people and general insufficient knowledge about the topics, almost 68% of the negotiating processes ends with a sub-optimal agreement, if compared with what could be achieved by a good negotiator.

There is much prejudice towards the figure of the negotiator who is commonly perceived as a negative person, able to subjugate the counterpart. On the contrary, it is necessary to comprehend that good communication skills and thorough knowledge of the topic are essential when looking for optimal results.

Before the negotiating process begins, the good negotiator should meditate on a few questions:

- Is it possible to make the environment in which the transaction will occur more comfortable?
- Is it possible to handle hostilities towards both people and the company represented?
- What can be considered the best communication method in order to guarantee the success of the negotiating process?

Given the above listed questions, it is necessary to understand that the most important skills of a negotiator are the communicative matrix and interpersonal relationship ability. Since negotiation takes place between two individuals, assertiveness towards the partner negotiator is important.

Therefore, it is necessary to seek a flexible method that can be applied to all those situations in which it is necessary to reach an agreement. The preferable skills that a good negotiator must show are objectivity with respect to transaction features, and bias which is useful to take apart the discussion.

The negotiation starts with the full awareness of the advantages of a particular idea or initiative, by at least one of the parties involved. The objective of the negotiation is to reach a fruitful exchange with the partner. For that reason, it is essential to create a sort of "empathy" in order to contain the potential areas of conflict of the counterpart. A further significant feature of the negotiating process is the perception of equality between the parties involved, thus reducing or excluding any form of hierarchy. The sharing and the involvement of psychological and emotional features of all the parties affect the transaction's effectiveness, in other words, the interpersonal relationship exerts a pivotal role. Even when there are emotionally-charged debates, the good negotiator should maintain a positive behavior together with providing accurate feedback to the counterpart.

Furthermore, it is necessary to identify accurately who will play the role of negotiator. The results achieved during the transactions depend on both the circumstances in which the negotiation happens, and the negotiator's skills.

The distinguishing features of a good negotiator are *curiosity*, *coherence*, *diplomacy*, *listening*, *empathy*, *proactivity*, *patience*, *flexibility*, *assertiveness*, and *introspection*.

The negotiator needn't manifest all those skills, but rather should be aware of the ones he/she needs to develop. Every single skill is crucial during the negotiating process, because each one is able to affect the negotiator's actions. The above-mentioned skills can be divided into three groups:

Practical skills: Curiosity, coherence, diplomacy;
Emotional skills: empathy, patience, listening, assertiveness.
Exchanging skills: introspection, flexibility, proactivity.

In addition to their general importance the role of the above cited groups of skills changes according to the different approaches to the negotiation: the distributive and the integrative [1-4].

Distributive Negotiation and Integrative Negotiation

The **distributive approach** occurs when a fixed amount of resources is available for the negotiation. In this circumstance, the individual goal is the ability to obtain the larger amount of resources in comparison to those obtainable by the counterpart. Even if the two parts at the end of the negotiation reach a perfect division of the resources, the result is suboptimal. For instance, if within a house there are only 6 oranges and two sisters want them, they may decide to divide the number of oranges into 3 for each sister. But if one of them needs 4 oranges to make a cake, she will be dissatisfied by the result of the negotiation, because she will not be able to reach her objective (make the cake). Despite being not completely satisfied, the use of a distributive approach to negotiation is a common choice, because it is often the only alternative, and because of the perception of victory felt by both sides.

Pruitt and Carnevale [5] provide four main strategies that can drive to a good performance during the distributive negotiation which are:

- Allow;
- Drop out of the negotiation;
- Inaction;
- Request.

Allow means reformulate the initial requests in favor of the counterpart. However, the reformulation must be reasonable if the task is a positive reaction to it. Weingart and colleagues [6] affirm that the correlation between concessions and negotiation results can be represented by a U shaped curve. The negotiation style may be fairly resolute. For each given concession, it is necessary to obtain a concession in turn.

Drop out of the negotiation is a common situation that takes place during the distributive negotiation, when the counterpart's proposals are not satisfying. The winner is the part that achieves the better status.

Inaction may be useful for several reasons. For example, a time of inaction is useful to elaborate a new strategy, or to stress the counterpart. The role of inaction tends to be extremely productive when the counterpart has a time limit to realize the transaction.

Request: this strategy indicates the proper way to ask for something to the counterpart, without offering any concession in exchange. Request includes challenging the counterpart, to press to obtain something and to attempt to persuade. Each of these actions implies a favorite position of the negotiator with respect to his counterpart.

The distributive negotiation leads to different results in terms of winnings and losses, creating the win-lose or the lose-lose scenarios [7]. The win-win result is achievable only by using the integrative approach. The "win" and the "loss" represent the perception that each side has before the negotiation. For instance, a "win" result occurs when the outcome of a negotiation is better than expected, while a "loss" is perceived when the outcome is worse than expected. Two people may receive the same outcome in measurable terms, for one side it may be a loss, while for the other it represents a win. In other words, expectations determine one's perception of any given result. Going into details in a win-lose scenario, both sides attempt to win, without taking into consideration the outcome of the other party. Both parties take part in the negotiation with energy, trying to obtain the best result, therefore only one side will perceive the outcome as positive. The win-lose outcomes are based on a principle of competition between participants. At the end of the process, each side gets part of what he or she wanted, thus obtaining a sub-optimal solution if compared with the result that could have been reached through an integrative approach. In a Win-Lose scenario, only one of the two parties (the Winner) attains the expected range of results. Similarly, one of the following situations may happen in a Lose-Lose scenario: either both parties concede bargaining positions outside their expected ranges, or no deal is reached. Both parties may end up in worse positions than when they started the negotiations. An example of this situation would be a budget-cutting negotiation in which all parties lose money. In some lose-lose situations, all parties understand that losses are unavoidable and that they will be distributed, which is preferable to win-lose outcomes because at least the distribution is considered fair.

The typical result of the *integrative approach* to the negotiation is the win-win scenario where both parts reach a satisfying agreement. In some cases, a win-win result indicates that a new solution was found, in order to improve the position of both parties. Outcomes occur when each side of a dispute feels it has won. Since both sides benefit from the win –win scenario, any resolution to the conflict is likely to be voluntarily accepted. In order to analyze deeply the integrative approach, we need to go back to the example of the oranges. In a house there are two sisters who need some oranges. The oranges are 6 and the sisters need to divide them. Following the distributive approach the sisters divide the oranges into two equal parts, but that solution is not satisfactory because one of them needs 4 oranges to make an orange cake. By following the integrative approach, if they try to explain their needs clearly, the probability to find a win-win solution increases. For example, if one sister needs the juice of the four oranges to make the orange cake, whereas the other one needs the peels of the oranges to make a liqueur, they may easily find an agreement.

The Integrative approach allows participants to reach satisfying results, by finding productive solutions.

In the following section of this chapter negotiation will be analyzed within the healthcare context. Since the '90s, the progressive attribution of administrative tasks to physicians has determined the need to negotiate over resources and budget assignment within organizations. Furthermore, physicians have been engaged in managerial roles, and have started to play a double role (as clinicians and as managers) in the workplace. For that reason, they have begun to negotiate internally in the attempt to balance time and commitment between the two roles.

The next section illustrates the contextual framework in which healthcare organizations assumed the configuration of a private corporation and physicians started to be in charge of managerial tasks.

NEW PUBLIC MANAGEMENT: THE SOURCE OF THE ADMINISTRATIVE TASKS FOR PHYSICIANS

In the '90s many Western countries radically reformed their public sector. The main implemented innovation in the public sector was the introduction of several managerial ideas and practices coming from the private sector. The above-cited process took the name of New Public Management [8, 9]. The New Public Management corresponds to a new managerial approach based on the need to achieve a good governance system, able to guarantee the attainment of high levels of efficacy and effectiveness in public action. During the '90s, the New Public management affected also the Italian public system, thus radically transforming the managerial principles of public organizations, including the healthcare sector. As a result, the Italian National health system has been influenced by profound changes aimed at improving the managerial approaches. Going into detail the 90s' legislative decrees created a system in which institutional rules have been substituted by technical ones. It is because of the complexity in the management of a modern healthcare organization based on the need to comply with both institutional and technical rules at the same time (see chapter one). Modern society asks for efficiency and effectiveness, which can be reached through the respect of technical requirements but it asks also for fairness, appropriateness and justice, a set of factors that represent institutional requirements.

Hospitals and healthcare organizations should show on the one hand the ability to operate effectively and efficiently, while on the other, they should be able to meet the needs expressed by society and by the population in general. Within these organizations, efficiency and effectiveness must be accompanied by a continuous demonstration of appropriateness and by complete legitimacy of the organization.

Healthcare managers have to face the challenge to act by respecting many different rules, using complex logic and tools.

Generally, in the 90s', the reforms stressed specific technical aspects of management such as cost control, financial transparency and the decentralization of management authority [10], together with implying new tasks and responsibilities not only for managers but also for healthcare professionals. Consequently, even within the healthcare sector, managers and professionals felt the need to acquire administrative and managerial guidelines that were unknown until that moment. Moreover, the reforms for healthcare professionals implied the redistribution of power, by shifting the emphasis from professional standards to measurable standards of performance recorded and monitored by innovative accounting systems [8, 11].

The main task of the new public management is efficiency, which can be achieved following different approaches. Firstly, the whole organization considered as a complex of human and organizational processes, needs to be designed or re-designed in a new way, based on an efficiency logic. It is necessary to develop a certain amount of competition between organizations in order to stress their productivity. Moreover, competitiveness and efficiency determine the need to increase the assumption of managerial and professional responsibilities. Physicians need to be more task- oriented and to assume administrative responsibilities besides the professional ones. Finally, it is essential to develop strong partnerships with the external stakeholders in order to build a systematic system of feedback on which continuous efficiency monitoring is based.

Literature provides a wide range of definitions of the New Public Management concept. For instance, Pollitt [12] affirms that the decision to develop the New Public Management approach within public administrations is based on the superiority of the private managerial approaches with respect to public ones. Ashburner [13] starts from a different point of view by stating that the New Public Management indicates a new concept of public services that use private managerial approaches without denying the identity of the public nature of organizations.

Generally, the New Public management can be considered a renovation of public administration. It is a new starting point for all the organizations operating in the public sector, including healthcare. Figure 1 provides reasons and operative tools of the New Public Management.

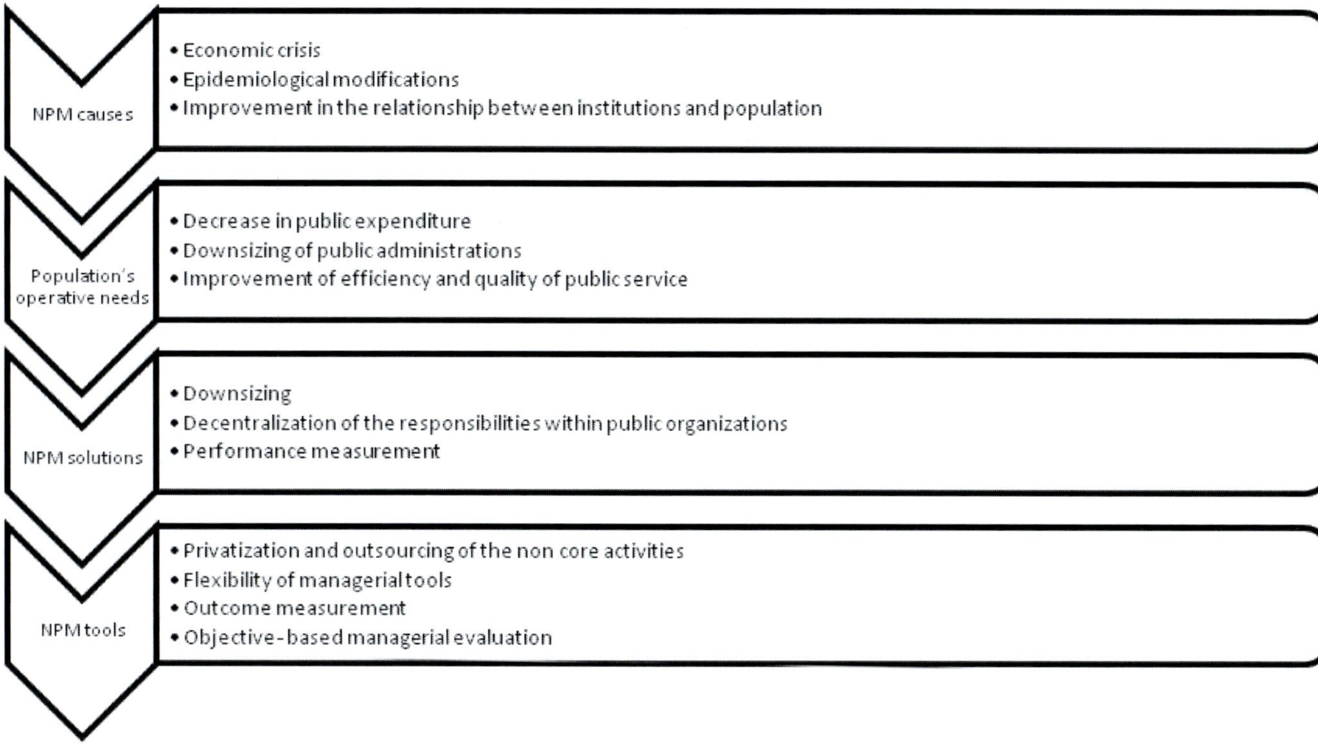

Figure 1. New public management steps.

As Figure 1 shows, NPM is the public organization's response to the developing needs of a changing population, taking into consideration the progressive lack of resources. People demanded streamlining on procedures together with a decrease in taxation. From this emerged the need to improve the efficiency in service provision. The solutions proposed by the NPM determined an increasing level of responsibility attributed to managers and healthcare professionals about their performance and operative tasks. In many situations, as in the healthcare sector, these needs have been translated in the attribution of administrative and managerial responsibilities to healthcare professionals, in order to downsize but also to decentralize the responsibilities from the top management to the operational level. The above-cited principles are the first step to comprehend how the new public management changed the organizational behavior of physicians and nurses staffed in public hospitals. Moreover, the NPM led to a progressive change in the role boundaries, thus affecting the internal balance between the health activities and administrative ones. Kitchener [14], for example, analyzes the confusion of UK physicians, who became clinical directors. Kurunmäki [15], who shows the hybridization of the healthcare profession, and the claim of responsibility on the administrative tasks operated by the accounting professionals, provides another interesting example of that condition. It can be stated that the attribution of new tasks and responsibilities, which exceed the physiological role of healthcare professionals, determines both an internal and an external negotiation. The first perspective of the negotiation process analyzes the physician's role conflicts due to their double level of responsibility as doctors and managers. In this case, the role of the negotiation affects the ability of physicians to accept the balance between these two conflicting roles. On the other hand, the second perspective of analysis of the negotiating process is externally oriented. It is focused on the development of the administrative activities attributed to doctors, which implies a systematic need to negotiate objectives, resources and responsibilities with employees, colleagues and supervisors. The next section is focused on the analysis of the two sides of negotiation within the healthcare context.

The Two Sides of Negotiation in Healthcare: The Internal and the External Involvement of Physicians

As previously claimed, there are two main perspectives through which it is possible to analyze how the negotiating processes occur within healthcare organizations. Due to the new managerial responsibilities assigned to physicians, they are now called to take on a larger number of roles than before. Besides their medical activities, they need to administrate economic, human and technological resources. The boundaries of their professions are extremely transient, thus generating role conflicts and confusion. Physicians need to negotiate internally to establish priorities on different tasks and at the same time they need to negotiate externally in order to obtain a large amount of resources. Literature provides some interesting examples on both perspectives.

The Internal Negotiation of Physicians: Role Conflict and Role Ambiguity

Contributions about the internal dynamics of negotiation reveal a common point when considering the difficulty manifested by physicians in accepting the change and in adapting themselves to the double role, introduced by the NPM. As affirmed by Kippist and Fitzgerald [16], the introduction of the hybrid roles determines a role conflict and the consciousness of a lack of competencies about managerial education, time pressures and personality factors. The main issue is related to the time distribution between managerial and clinical activities. Due to their hybrid roles, physicians perceive that they spend a lot of time in their managerial tasks, and have less time to dedicate to their main clinical role [17, 18]. Medical management implies the construction of roles in which medicine and management need to be mediated by a single person, who has to check the delivery of healthcare according to a fixed budget, the performance review and the risk management in addition to normal care activities [19].

Besides the *role conflict* (see box 1) experienced by physicians, the unbalanced allocation of time between the two activities causes further internal conflicts. The natural predisposition of physicians to solve firstly the clinical activities, and then the managerial ones, produces an inevitable delay in the work plan. The mentioned inconvenience can generate both a lack of satisfaction and conflicts with other members of the organization, who need to receive answers and directions from their "manager." In other words, it is the *role ambiguity* (see box 1) through which an individual is not able to understand the expectations of the remaining cooperators.

Box 1. Role conflict and role ambiguity [20, 1]

Role conflict: role conflict occurs when people disagree about the expectations for a given role or when someone has difficulty satisfying the expectations because the duties are unclear, complicated, or disagreeable. The result is that the individual staffed in the conflicting role is confused about the ways of satisfying the different expectations. Conflicts among the professional roles begin because of both the human's desire to reach success, and the pressure exerted on him by two imposing and incompatible demands. The individual may find himself/herself pulled in various directions as he/she tries to respond to the different statuses he/she holds. Role conflict can assume two different connotations depending on what the object of the conflict is. For example, when the roles are associated with two different statuses, the result is status strain, while when the conflicting roles are both associated with the same status, the result is known as role strain. The most obvious example of role conflict is the work/family conflict, which occurs when one feels pulled between familial and professional obligations. Habitually women are the most exposed to those conflicts, due to their dual role in society. For example, a mother who is also a manager has to work long hours at the office, sometimes during the weekend, circumstances which take her away from her children. Men can also be subjected to role conflicts, for example a single man may be in conflict with working hours and his free time. For instance, a man who is a teacher and a father can be asked by the school board and parents to spend most of his after-school hours on meetings and additional educational activities with students whereas his family expects him to spend evenings at home. It is a case of role conflict since the man is unable to satisfy both of these incompatible expectations. The feeling of people who experience these situations is characterized by distress and dissatisfaction.

Corresponding to a role conflict there are several expectations toward the same person, instead when there is role ambiguity it means that the "role designer" was not able to clearly define what tasks concern a given role. Role ambiguity denotes uncertainty about expectations, behaviors, and consequences associated with a given role.

An individual needs to know others' expectations of the rights, duties, and responsibilities of the role exerted in order to operate properly. Furthermore, the behavior that will lead to both the fulfillment of those expectations, and its consequences, is a main factor to be aware of in the workplace. Role ambiguity results when organizational factors (e.g., rapidly changing organizational structures, job feedback systems) and individual factors (e.g., information processing biases) are non-existent or inadequately communicated. A job description is an example of a formal organizational mechanism that may alleviate role ambiguity. Role ambiguity is positively correlated with both anxiety and intention to leave (the role), and negatively correlated with organizational commitment, employee involvement, and job satisfaction.

Tengelin and colleagues [21] offer an interesting example of both role conflict and role ambiguity. They used interviews performed with clinical managers to provide a general view about how they try to solve the problem of the time balancing. An interesting contribution is provided by the story of a physician who has been suddenly called to assume the direction of the ward where he has been working for many years. A strong role conflict between what he would like to do (the doctor), and what the managerial board expects from him (to be the ward manager) affects his work commitment together with a strong role ambiguity that emerges from the expectations that his colleagues have on him. They would appreciate his help as was the case before the new managerial responsibilities without considering the total change of his tasks.

"*... I know the work very well, I know what is being done at the ward and so, but it is also hard to detach from that. Subordinates might expect me to do the things I did before* (as a physician)... *I was very harsh on that from the beginning, that I will not do that kind of work. I made myself clear, because if I started to help in these kinds of selected efforts, then I would do it every day. Now it is rare that I help out, and if I do, it is necessary, during crisis.... They have to solve themselves..*"

In this passage of the interview, it is clear that is extremely hard for the physician to keep providing his clinical skills, due to the additional managerial tasks in which he has been enrolled. Every day: "*When we gather at the morning meeting and say to each other "wow, there is a lot to do today" I don't say that I can go ...*"

Although it seems that physicians make the decision to perform or not to perform clinical activities, Kippist and Fitzgerald [16] demonstrate that it is not always possible for them to choose to not be involved in clinical activities. It is because there are several constraints, which can influence the decision of physicians in their daily routine. The first constraint is the nature of the clinical activities: a medical emergency cannot be scheduled or postponed, even in presence of previously planned managerial activities. Secondly, the priority attributed to the managerial activities relies on the physician's opinion If the degree of interest is low, physician may prioritize the clinical activities in spite of the managerial ones. Finally, a third critical constraint is the role exerted by individual values. As stated in chapter four, physicians need to develop and to fulfill their values through their activities to be very satisfied. Therefore, if their work is more oriented to the intrinsic values (creativity, training), than to the extrinsic ones (earning, career), their double role is stronger on the clinical side rather than on the managerial side.

Although most of the contributions are incline to stress the confusion and the dissatisfaction related to the double role of physicians, Doolin [22], analyzing the experience of the healthcare reform in New Zealand, provides a different side of the story. The author tends to appreciate the double role of physicians, declaring that the clinical managers are progressively adapting their work-life to the new commercial tasks imposed by the healthcare sector. He affirms that even assuming new managerial skills, the real nature of clinical managers is always based on their clinical side, which allows them to retain credibility with other clinicians [22-24]. The author states that the assumption of new managerial responsibilities is not a de-professionalization, but rather a renegotiation of the boundaries between medicine and management. The "New" physician is able to be a mediator, who transmits norms and values of the managerial culture into medicine. With this perspective, we can affirm that physicians do not always negatively perceive their position with regards to their additional managerial role. They definitely need to perform an internal negotiation, in order to be able to interpret their double role.

Moving now to the external approach to negotiation, the following paragraph analyzes the increase of the administrative responsibilities attributed to physicians, together with their involvement in negotiating processes, which are essential to obtain resources. In this second perspective the style and the goals that physicians reach through negotiation, have been considered.

The External Side of Negotiation: Physicians' Engagement during Budget Meetings

The internal perspective of the negotiation is focused on the commitment and acceptation that physicians develop about the double role constraints, whereas the analysis of the external perspective aims at exploring the behavior of physicians when they are called to negotiate.

One of the most common events of negotiation is represented by the budget discussion in which physicians, especially those engaged in managerial roles, are frequently involved.

Literature on this topic approaches the problem following different perspectives. Fisher and colleagues [25], thanks to an experimental study explore the effect of negotiation on the economic conditions of the budget. Their attention is particularly focused on the results of the negotiating processes starting from the analysis of the initial approach of the counterparts. They claim that the higher the initial position of the parts, the lower the ability to make concessions to the counterparts. Therefore, it confirms what we have shown during the analysis of the distributive negotiation. Authors observe a different level of information about the expected behavior of the counterpart through the analysis of the relationship between superiors and subordinates. Frequently, subordinates are more conscious than the superiors about the strategic behaviors adopted during the negotiation, because subordinates may have observed their superiors many times during the past. Fisher and colleagues [26] who analyzed the time effects of the negotiating processes, provide a further significant contribution. They take into consideration the effect that prior negotiations exert on successive negotiation strategies and outcomes. While during the first negotiation the parts are more prone to protect their position in order to win the negotiation, during the following opportunities the agreement increases. The length of the interaction seems to affect the cooperation between individuals [26] and it is possible to observe an integrative approach to the negotiation related to past or future relationships, due to a more collaborative approach adopted by the parts.

Finally, there are some exogenous constraints, which can exert a role on negotiations. Arnold [27] affirms that economic conditions but also financial pressures may have an impact on the budget discussion, determining a more collaborative approach between superiors and subordinates. The collaboration starts from the application of a centralized approach to the discussion in presence of constraints, whereas the approach applied in absence of constraints is participative. In this second perspective of analysis, what it is important is the style adopted during the negotiation, but also the circumstances in which the process occurs. Even for the external approach to the negotiation, evidence concerning Italian physicians is provided in the following pages.

THE DOUBLE SIDE OF NEGOTIATION: EVIDENCE FROM ITALIAN PHYSICIANS

In order to illustrate the negotiation perspectives above cited, we provide a semi-structured questionnaire. Our aim is to provide a survey of the physician's perception of hybrid roles together with a description of their negotiating style. Table 1 provides a brief overview of the section contents, their references, the methods employed to survey data and finally the results interpretation instructions.

Table 1. Questionnaire overview and details

Part detail	Content	References	Method	Results interpretation
AREA A				
1 (Section A)	Role conflicts	Rizzo and colleagues [20]	The surveyed physician is asked to answer to each question indicating the degree of agreement to each statement on the basis of a four point Likert scale. Value 1 indicates a strongly disagreement with the statement, while value 4 a strongly agreement.	The higher is the final rating, the higher is the role conflict.

Table 1. (Continued)

Part detail	Content	References	Method	Results interpretation
1 (Section B)	Role ambiguities		Surveyed physician is asked to answer to each question indicating the degree of agreement to each statement on the basis of a four point Likert scale. Value 1 indicates a strongly disagreement with the statement, while value 4 a strongly agreement.	The lower is the final rating of the section B, the higher is the ambiguity of role.
2	Time commitment	Tenglein and colleagues [21]	Questions have been formulated following a mixed method approach in order to catch the perception of time wasting and time fragmentation. Moreover they explore how the time is allocated in respect to the different activities and which are the most confounding areas.	The higher is the final rating resulting from questions 1,2,3, the higher is the perception of a wrong time commitment. Questions 4,5 and 6 provide qualitative information about time commitment.

Part detail	Content	References	Method	Results interpretation
3	Double role	Kippist and Fitzgerald [16]. Llewellyn [19]	Questions have been formulated following a mixed method approach in order to catch the perception that physicians have relatively to their mediating role between clinical and administrative activities. Some questions are finalized to qualitatively explore the barriers and the results of the internal negotiation of physicians in the attempt to perform both activities.	The higher is the final rating resulting from questions 1-6, the higher is the level of comfort with the double role played. Questions 7 and 8 provide qualitative information about double role.
AREA B				
A	Passivity	Morandi, [28].	Questions have been formulated in order to determine the presence of particular "automatism" during the negotiating processes.	The higher is the final rating the stronger is the automatism of Passivity.
B	Aggressiveness			The higher is the final rating the stronger is the automatism of Aggressiveness.

Table 1. (Continued)

Part detail	Content	References	Method	Results interpretation
C	Arrogance		The Surveyed physician is asked to answer to each question by indicating the degree of agreement to each statement using a four point Likert scale from 1 = strongly disagree to 4 = strongly agree.	The higher is the final rating the stronger is the automatism of Arrogance.
D	Distress			The higher is the final rating the stronger is the automatism of Distress.
E	Fatalism			The higher is the final rating the stronger is the automatism of Fatalism.

Questionnaire and Survey Strategy

Two pools of questions (Area A: the internal side of negotiation, Area B: the external side of negotiation) were developed in order to explore the physician's perception of the topic. The first section gathers the personal data of respondents. Another nine sections complete the questionnaire[5]. We developed a preliminary version of the questionnaire and after a first round of reviews, we decided to pre-test the questionnaire on physicians enrolled in managerial positions. Later we decided to distribute the questionnaire to 12 physicians staffed in managerial positions in Italian hospitals. Our sample was skilled in value scale construction, HR practices in healthcare organizations, managerial and organizational tasks. All physicians attended a MBA Program in Management of healthcare organizations between 2013 and 2015.

[5] The whole questionnaire is available upon request to the Author.

Demographic Features of the Sample

The sample of 12 physicians is composed of 5 public health specialists, 2 gynecologists; 1 specialist in psychiatry, 1 radiologist, 1 cardiologist and 1 surgeon. Three of the sampled physicians are Clinical directors, 4 are Heads of a complex ward unit, one is in charge of a simple ward unit, and three are Clinical managers. Five of the sampled physicians are male while the majority of them are female. The mean value of their age is 46 years old, while their managerial tenure in 3.7 years (mean value). About their involvement in budget discussions, the sample goes from a minimum of one opportunity to negotiate, to 11 budget discussions. Finally, the most part of the sample was involved in less than five negotiations during the previous year.

Questionnaire Results

The Internal Side of Negotiation

The first area of the questionnaire regards the role of conflict inspection. The main aim of this section is to explore if with the assumption of managerial responsibilities physicians started to perceive a disagreement about the expectations for their role. Also, they may not feel able to satisfy expectations, because their duties are unclear, extremely complicated, or disagreeable.

Table 2 provides the results obtained thanks to this area of the questionnaire by showing the distribution of the answers among the four levels of agreement with the statements. The bold percentages are the highest ones.

The statement preceding all the items was: "*Since I have assumed managerial responsibilities*"

The majority of our respondents agree that their daily activities could be done in different ways. Moreover, they agree on the lack of guidelines able to drive them, and even when the directives are there, they are vague. They receive assignments but without real authority to enforce them and without adequate resources and materials to execute them. Often the groups working together are different and consequently, there are different requests and expectations from them. At the same time, they don't always agree on the incompatibility of the rules under which they have to work, and they do not feel the need to fight against the rules to carry out an assignment. Finally, they don't believe in the uselessness of their activities and in the disagreement among their staff members on the activities performed.

Since as we remember value 1 indicates a strong disagreement with the statement, while value 4 a strong agreement, by analyzing the general mean of the questionnaire we can observe the following situation. Five of the sampled physicians agree with the majority of the items that means a medium level of role conflict (the mean of each of their questionnaires is about 3). Four physicians are low in the role conflict, the mean of their answers is between 1 and 2, and finally two of the sampled physicians show a high agreement with the statements, indicating the highest level of role conflict. The mean of their questionnaires is around 4.

Table 2. Role conflict answers

Items	Strongly disagree (%)	Disagree (%)	Agree (%)	Strongly agree (%)
I have to do things that should be done differently	0	17	**83**	0
Lack of policies and guidelines to help me	0	33	**50**	17
I work under incompatible policies and guidelines	0	**67**	17	16
I receive assignments without having the necessary manpower to complete them	0	0	**67**	33
I have to buck a rule or policy in order to carry out an assignment	0	**67**	16	17
I have to "feel my way" in performing my duties	1	33	33	33
I work with two or more groups who operate quite differently	0	33	**50**	17
I receive incompatible requests from two or more people	1	33	33	33
I do things that are apt to be accepted by one person and not accepted by the remaining staff members	0	**67**	16	17
I receive an assignment without adequate resources and materials to execute it	0	0	**67**	33
I work on unnecessary things	0	**67**	17	16
I have to work under vague directives and orders	0	16	**67**	17

Table 3. Role ambiguity answers

Items	Strongly disagree (%)	Disagree (%)	Agree (%)	Strongly agree (%)
I feel confident because of my increased authority	0	**50**	33	17
Goals and objectives are planned and clear to me	0	**67**	33	0
I am able to act individually regardless of the group I work with	17	33	**50**	0
I know that I'm managing my time properly	0	33	**67**	0
I know what my responsibilities are	0	17	**83**	0
I have to "feel my way" in performing my duties (reverse coded)	18	**34**	18	30
I'm certain about a raise or promotion evaluation criteria	0	**67**	33	0
I'm provided with a proper amount of work	0	33	**67**	0
I know exactly what is expected of me	1	33	33	33
Explanations on what has to be done are clear	0	**100**	0	0
I perform a work that suits my values	0	0	**83**	17
Everyone is aware of my role, duties and competences	0	**50**	33	17

The second area of the questionnaire concerns role ambiguity. Its main aim is to explore if with the assumption of managerial responsibilities physicians are uncertain about the expectations, behaviors, and consequences associated with their new role. In presence of role ambiguity, the individual ignores what the expectations about his role are.

Table 3 provides the results of this area of the survey by showing the how the answers are distributed in percentages; the bold percentages are the highest ones.

The statement preceding all the items was: "Since I have assumed managerial responsibilities"

The majority of our respondents disagree on the confidence with the increased authority, and with the clarity of the goals and objectives assigned. All respondents affirm that the explanations about what has to be done are unclear. They are uncertain about the evaluation criteria used for the raise and for the promotion. The majority of physicians claim that their colleagues and subordinates are not aware of their role. Despite general confusion about their work schedule, sampled physicians show a high degree of autonomy in their work. They declare that they are able to act individually, and to have the right amount of work. They are conscious of time management and their responsibilities. Finally, the majority of them say that the work suits their values.

As for the previous section, even here value 1 indicates a strong disagreement with the statement. By analyzing the results obtained through the questionnaires we can observe that 5 physicians are low in the role ambiguity (the majority of their answers are concentrated around the disagreement with almost all the items). Three of the sampled physicians agree with the majority of the items, which indicates a medium level of role ambiguity. Finally, 3 of the sampled physicians show high agreement with the statements, indicating the highest level of role ambiguity.

The aim of the third part of the questionnaire is to analyze the time allocation of physicians enrolled in managerial activities. This section is composed of both open questions and multiple-choice questions. The answers show that, generally, physicians are not confused about how to allocate time between clinical and managerial activities. Moreover, they are not afraid about wasting time and time fragmentation. In a global perspective, although physicians staffed in managerial roles need to perform both clinical and managerial activities, they feel they are able to properly distribute their work time.

Notwithstanding the comforting results of the questionnaire, it is interesting to identify what are considered time wasting activities. The "administrative tasks" are indicated as the most time wasting activities by 33% of the sampled physicians, while the remaining indicated as time wasting activities: the management of the allied staff (17%), the ICT systems development and implementation (16%); the research activities (16%); personal interests (14%). Table 4, which shows the list of daily activities the sampled physicians are involved in, provides further significant results. The activities were graded according to the frequency with which they have been cited. The last column indicates the average time that is usually dedicated to each daily activity.

Table 4. Daily activities grading and time allocation

Grading position	Activity	Citations frequency	Time allocation (within daily working time, that has to be considered as 100% of the time available)
1°	*Interacting with employees*	6	25%
2°	*Participating in clinical practice*	4	47.5%
2°	*Fulfilling administrative duties*	4	17.5%
3°	*Taking active part in strategic networks*	3	8.3%
3°	*Data elaboration*	3	31.7%
4°	*Critical pathways development*	1	20%
4°	*Managing relationships with patients, relatives and institutions*	1	35%
4°	*Patients surveillance*	1	5%
4°	*Consulting*	1	10%

As Table 4 shows, sampled physicians declare that the interaction with employees takes just 25% (mean value) of their daily working time, although it was indicated as the most frequent activity in which they are involved (6 physicians indicated the interactions in the first position of the grading). The second most frequent activity is the participation in clinical practice. It takes up 47% of the total working time available. The surveillance of patients requires just 5% of the time. We can presume that the clinical activity involves, in addition to patient's care, the research activities and the meetings necessary to provide care. Moreover, it is interesting to notice that 35% of the time is dedicated to the relationship with patients, their relatives and the institutions, while 20% of the time is spent developing and elaborating critical pathways. The administrative duties employ 17% of the daily working time of physicians enrolled in managerial roles, whereas data elaboration requires approximately 32% of the time. Besides the relationships with patients, relatives and institutions, physicians pay attention to the strategic networks maintained with other physicians or research centers, to which they dedicate the 8% of their working time. Finally, consulting activities take up 10% of the time, and they correspond to the part of work dedicated to exchanging information about complex patients.

Table 5. No schedulable daily activities

Grading position	Activity	Citations frequency
1°	*Interactions with colleagues, employees and managers*	6
2°	*Managing relationship with patients, relatives and institutions*	5
3°	*Taking active part in strategic networks*	4
3°	*Fulfilling administrative duties*	4
4°	*Participating in clinical practice*	3

When considering time management, it is clear that some activities cannot be scheduled a priori, not being completely formalized, which means that their duration and time limits are not completely clear. Table 5 provides a list of those activities, which are organized depending on the frequency with which they have been indicated by respondents.

Interactions and relationships can scarcely be scheduled. Physicians indicated them as not fully describable in terms of limits and duration. On the other hand, in the middle of the ranking are situated the participation to strategic networks and the fulfilling of administrative activities, which can be scheduled. Finally, our sample declared that clinical practice is at the lowest level of the non-scheduling activities, probably due to the permanent hospital's timetable concerning patients' visits and consultancies.

The fourth section of the questionnaire is focused on the exploration of the mediating role of physicians. It is helpful in order to understand how physicians interpret their managerial roles, thus creating a real connection between the managerial and the clinical worlds. The questionnaire section is composed of both open questions and closed ones. Table 6 provides the results pertaining to this area of the questionnaire showing the percentages with which the answers are distributed, the bold percentages represents the highest ones.

All the items were preceded by the statement: "Since I have assumed managerial responsibilities."

As we can observe in Table 6, the majority of the answers indicate a general disagreement about the ability of the sampled physicians to mediate the role between managerial and clinical tasks. They that claim they're not playing the role of mediators between clinicians and managers. Even being enrolled in managerial roles, our sampled physicians do not perceive the opportunity to observe the entire functioning of the hospital and to become the "voice" with the Board of direction. They are not confident with the administrative activities; on the contrary they still perceive the changes implemented as an intrusion of the managerial activities in the clinical role. Despite being convinced about their ability to convey the significance of their clinical skills in a set of ideas belonging to management, they still give priority to the clinical work. We asked them to indicate some barriers considered to be the main obstacles to a good performance of the double role. Table 7 indicates how physicians have ranked these barriers.

Table 6. Physicians mediating role

Items	Strongly disagree (%)	Disagree (%)	Agree (%)	Strongly agree (%)
My role is helpful to improve the communication between managers and clinicians	19	**40**	25	16
I have the opportunity to observe the entire functioning of the hospital and to be the "voice" with the Board of direction	**40**	18	25	17
I'm progressively feeling confident with the world of business and profit, and I see myself as an entrepreneur of healthcare.	9	**50**	33	8
I'm able to convey the significance of my clinical skills in a set of ideas belonging to management	16	16	**51**	17
The feeling of intrusion of the managerial activities on my clinical role is very strong (reverse coded)	18	**40**	17	25
I continue to give priority to the clinical work (reverse coded)	14	19	**40**	27

Table 7. Double role barriers ranking

Rate	Activity
1°	*Lack of time*
2°	*Unpredictability of clinical tasks and consequent interference in the managerial ones*
3°	*Lack of managerial education*
4°	*Lack of interest in managerial tasks*

They affirm that the perception of the time lacking is the main barrier to carry out a good double role performance, while the second one is related to the unpredictability of the clinical tasks that can suspend the managerial activities (in terms of available time). Physicians are not completely confident about their managerial education, which is perceived as the third barrier, while the lack of interest in managerial tasks is placed in the last position. Table 7 shows a general effort of physicians at playing the double role assigned.

By summarizing the results coming from the first area of the questionnaire, we can affirm that the majority of the sampled physicians are subject to conflicting roles. They do not perceive the incompatibility of their roles, but they are often exposed to incompatible requests coming from working groups. They have specific responsibilities but they do not have the adequate tools and resources to deal with them.

Physicians feel they are exposed to role ambiguity. They perceive a lack of instructions and information, useful to play their double role. However, they are aware of their responsibilities, time constraints and autonomy, which means that the role ambiguity comes from the organizational context and not from personal uncertainties.

About the ability to balance time, the sampled physicians consider the administrative tasks as the most time wasting activity, even if they take up just 17% of their working time. On the contrary, the clinical practice absorbs 47.5% of the physicians working time. Clinical tasks are not considered wasting time activities, as they are for administrative ones. Both administrative activities and clinical practice have been indicated at the lowest level of the non-scheduling activities. It means that the time wasting activities have not been chosen based on the quantity of time needed to perform them, or on the possibility to schedule them, but rather the personal interest in the activity itself. Finally, physicians' indications on the barriers that impede the performance of their double role, are more related to the circumstances in which the work is performed (lack of time or impossibility to predict clinical activities), than to the personal abilities or interests of physicians.

The External Side of Negotiation

The following five areas of the questionnaire are focused on the exploration of the external side of negotiation and they are useful to understand physicians' behavior during the negotiating processes.

Table 8. Passivity trait

Items	Strongly disagree (%)	Disagree (%)	Agree (%)	Strongly agree (%)
My interest in negotiation is strictly related to a need, but it's not my own specific interest	0	33	**50**	17
I'm more prone to escape from an arduous situation than to improve my efforts to obtain my goals	33	**50**	17	0
Notwithstanding my appreciation for success, I often perceive that obstacles can brake me	0	**50**	33	17
I'm a smiling and kind person. It can cause the risk of being dominated by others	0	**83**	17	0
I'm aware of being too passive and obedient, but I really don't know how I can change my behavior	16.5	**67**	16.5	0
I'm more prone to be dominated by the happenings than to drive them. It represents an obstacle to the achievement of my goals.	17	**83**	0	0
I'm considered a kind and charming person	0	33	**50**	17
My friends and colleagues trust me, but often my behavior is source of astonishment and diffidence	0	**83**	17	0
I'm introverted and when I achieve success in a negotiation, it is due to fate and to the atmosphere and not to my personal abilities during the transactions	33	**67**	0	0

The first area is focused on the passivity trait. Table 8 provides the results coming from this passage of the questionnaire. For each question the frequency with which answers have been provided is given at the different levels of agreement. The bold values represent the highest percentages.

All the items were preceded by the statement: "During the negotiating process in which I'm involved"

Table 9. Aggressiveness trait

Items	Strongly disagree (%)	Disagree (%)	Agree (%)	Strongly agree (%)
I have high determination and when I have to face a negotiation I want to win	0	0	**83**	17
I am an extrovert. During the negotiating process I 'm more intent on protecting my point of view than to listen to my interlocutor	17	**83**	0	0
I'm not available to accept criticism and whenever it happens I get angry and narrow-minded. The tone of my voice increases and I speak a lot and very quickly.	0	**83**	17	0
My aggressiveness is a consequence of weakness but I don't know how to face it.	17	**83**	0	0
Frequently and without a real reason, I become withdrawn and mistrusting. I'm suspicious of my interlocutor and I constantly try to identify whether he/she is trying to cheat me	0	**83**	17	0
Attack is the best defense. I perceive the achievement of a minimum advantage as a victory	17	**83**	0	0
I pay attention to my interlocutor's speech just to catch the best moment to speak	0	**83**	17	0
I underestimate the psychological features of my interlocutor and pay attention to the strong points of the negotiating process	0	**83**	17	0
I'm very dynamic, but it is mainly due to a nervous reaction	17	**83**	0	0

Although the sampled physicians declare that their interest in negotiation is strictly related to a need, they seem to face negotiations by playing an active role. They show a systematic disagreement with the majority of the items. Surveyed physicians declare that they are not afraid of arduous situations, and that they are able to surpass the obstacles. They do not perceive the risk of being dominated by others. On the contrary, they claim to be charming and smiling people. The average of the results is around value 2, indicating a low level of passivity.

The aim of the following area is to survey the degree of aggressiveness during the negotiating processes. Table 9 provides the list of the items and the distribution of the answers together with the level of agreement or disagreement with the affirmations. The bold values represent the highest percentages.

The statement preceding all the items was: "*During the negotiating process in which I'm involved.*"

As previously noticed, even for the aggressiveness trait, the sampled physicians show a systematic disagreement with the items, which indicates a low level of aggressiveness. Although they initially comply with the statement "I have high determination and when I have to face negotiation I want to win," they declare afterwards that they take into consideration the point of view of the interlocutors, besides trying to figure out the right moment to speak. Surveyed physicians are open-minded in the workplace and they positively accept criticism from the counterpart. Taking into consideration the average result of each statement, that may vary between 1 that indicates strong disagreement with the statement and 4 which corresponds to high agreement, we observe that all of them are concentrated between the values 1 and 2, confirming the lack of aggressiveness among physicians during the negotiating processes.

The following section of the questionnaire is dedicated to the analysis of the presence of the arrogance trait among the surveyed physicians, taking into consideration the negotiating processes. Table 10 provides the answers collected for each item by showing how they are distributed among the level of agreement. The bold values indicate the highest percentages.

All the items were preceded by the statement: "*During the negotiating process in which I'm involved.*"

When analyzing the arrogance trait, the sampled physicians declare they are scarcely arrogant during the negotiating process. They do not agree about their lack of ability to achieve results through negotiation, and they feel responsible for the good or bad results achieved. They declare they are more interested in the transaction results, than on the ability to fascinate their counterpart. The sampled physicians are convinced of not being arrogant, but rather they perceive themselves as good speakers. Taking into consideration the general average resulting from the questionnaire (as above ranging between 1 and 4), two respondents attested their answers around the value 3, indicating a medium degree of arrogance, the rest of the physicians are concentrated between values 1 and 2 thus declaring a low level of arrogance during the negotiating process.

The fourth area concerning the external side of negotiation analyzes the level of distress that can affect the negotiating process.

Table 10. Arrogance trait

Items	Strongly disagree (%)	Disagree (%)	Agree (%)	Strongly agree (%)
I feel confident of my skills and I think I am talented for the transactions. I like the negotiation very much, but the results achieved are worse than what I expected	0	**67**	33	0
I face the situations with an intimate pleasure that often may result irritating for my interlocutors and of which I'm not always aware.	17	**83**	0	0
Often I'm distressed and I'm prone to fool the interlocutor	**50**	**50**	0	0
I'm a very good speaker and even my silences are supposed to communicate	0	16.5	**67**	16.5
I'm very self-oriented and I don't take into consideration the needs and the psychological traits of my interlocutors	33	**50**	17	0
When the transaction presents a negative result, it seems that I do not care. Actually I feel really angry with my counterpart who doesn't give in to my fashion and intelligence	0	**67**	33	0
I'm prone to attribute the responsibility for the failure of negotiating process to my counterpart	0	**67**	33	0
If it fails, I immediately try to change the interlocutor, hoping that he/she will be better than the previous one	0	**67**	33	0
My attitude is very extroverted. Often I'm too confident about the transaction and I risk appearing arrogant	17	**50**	33	0

Table 11. Distress trait

Items	Strongly disagree (%)	Disagree (%)	Agree (%)	Strongly agree (%)
Whenever I have to meet an interlocutor, although I'm not usually introvert, my introversion increases	0	**50**	**50**	0
At the beginning of the discussion I lose clarity of mind and my distress increases	0	**100**	0	0
It is very hard to gather my thoughts because I'm not able to communicate clearly	17	**83**	0	0
My listening skills are very good (it is one of my points of strength), but I'm not able to step in at the right moment (it is one of my points of weakness)	16.5	**67**	16.5	0
I try to conclude it in a hurry and my counterpart immediately understands it	16.5	**67**	16.5	0
Sometimes I feel uncomfortable	**50**	0	**50**	0
Although I'm an open minded person, I tend to become aggressive to react to the distress of the negotiation	0	**67**	33	0
My ability in the transaction is often damaged by distress	15	**50**	20	15
Through his/her questions I understand that my interlocutor perceives my distress	0	**83**	17	0

Table 11 provides the answers collected for each item. The bold values indicate the highest percentages on the agreement or disagreement of the presence of distress.

All the items were preceded by the statement: "*During the negotiating process in which I'm involved.*"

The sampled physicians show a low level of distress during the negotiating processes. They are confident about their ability to communicate; they do not feel the damage of distress and of the resulting aggressiveness. In the physicians' opinion, distress is not perceptible. The results of the questionnaire confirm a low perception of the distress trait during the negotiating processes. The average of the results is between level 1 and 2, indicating a general disagreement with the statements, and consequently a low level of distress.

The last trait inspected concerns the fatalism perceived by physicians during the negotiating processes in which they are involved. Table 12 presents the distribution of the answers collected for each item. The bold values indicate the highest percentages.

All the items were preceded by the statement: "*During the negotiating process in which I'm involved.*"

Table 12. Fatalism trait

Items	Strongly disagree (%)	Disagree (%)	Agree (%)	Strongly agree (%)
I am not able to find automatically the reason behind the negotiation. My behavior is introverted and emotionally unstable. In my opinion negotiation is boring and pedantic	**100**	0	0	0
Since I don't want to expose myself, I prefer to avoid situations where I have to negotiate.	17	**83**	0	0
I prefer to avoid the risk of defeat. For that reason I try to escape those negotiations where there is a low probability of success	0	**83**	17	0
The fear about the unknown makes me diffident and doubtful about the whole process	0	**83**	17	0
I'm ironic	0	33	**67**	0
My behavior is not enthusiastic and often my interlocutor interprets it as an irritating attitude of comfort	17	**50**	33	0
Sometimes I try to overcome my fatalism	0	**50**	**50**	0
Due to my fatalism when the negotiation ends negatively, I think: "well it ended as I had thought"	0	**83**	17	0
I think that external features can influence my success in the transaction	0	16.5	**67**	16.5

Table 13. The negotiator's traits: a comparative view

ID	Passivity	Aggressiveness	Arrogance	Distress	Fatalism
1	2	2.1	2.2	2.2	2.2
2	2.4	2.4	2.7	2.4	2.6
3	2.3	2.1	2.2	2.3	2.1
4	2.2	2.1	2.3	1.7	1.9
5	2.1	1.9	1.8	2	2.1
6	2.2	2.1	1.9	2	2.1
7	2.5	1.5	2.2	1.5	2.1
8	2	2	3.3	1.7	3
9	2.2	2.1	2.3	2	2.5
10	2.5	2.2	2.4	2.1	2.3
11	2.3	2.4	3	2.2	2
12	2	1.6	2.5	1.8	2.1

All respondents agreed about their interest in negotiation, which is not considered a boring activity. They are prone to face risks and to be involved even in uncertain negotiations. Although they are not fatalists when negotiations reach negative results, they are prone to think that the external context influenced the outcome.

By analyzing the average of the results achieved (ranking from 1 to 4), we observe that just two respondents consider themselves as fatalists during the negotiating process. The remaining physicians show lower levels of agreement with the statement, thus indicating that they cannot be considered as being fatalists.

By analyzing the external features of negotiations and considering all traits, the sampled physicians seem to be well balanced. It is not essential that all traits coexist in each person, whereas it is significantly probable that each physician manifests several traits contextually as can be seen in Table 13.

As we can observe, several traits have become known for each respondent, thus indicating the possibility to contextually recognize more than one trait in a single person. For instance, ID 1 presents similar results, when comparing all the traits, whereas ID 8 presents high traits of arrogance and fatalism. Finally, ID 12 is higher in arrogance than in the remaining traits.

The results analyzed in this chapter prove empirically that physicians enrolled into managerial roles are playing in both internal oriented and external oriented negotiating processes.

CONCLUSION

This chapter focused on one of the most important organizational behavioral conducts: negotiation. Starting from a brief exploration of the role of the negotiator, this chapter analyzes two main negotiating strategies: integrative and distributive. Negotiation is extremely relevant within healthcare organizations because it is one of the new managerial activities attributed to physicians by the New Public Management. From the beginning of the '90s, physicians have been involved in negotiating processes, as for instance, in budgeting discussions. They started to be involved in double and often conflicting roles: administrative and clinical. The analysis of the negotiation process takes into consideration the perception of physicians with respect to both their ability to negotiate internally and externally.

We performed a survey by administering a semi- structured questionnaire to 12 physicians in managerial roles. The analysis of the internal side of negotiation reveals that physicians are experiencing a role conflict between clinical and administrative duties. They think that the guidelines for their work are not clear and consequently, they find it hard to face the work routine. Our surveyed physicians receive assignments that they are not able to perform due to a lack of resources and tools, which can lead to patient, colleague and manager dissatisfaction. Moreover it may generate the feeling of being pulled in different directions. Surveyed physicians seem to be less affected by the role ambiguity and even if they perceive a lack of clarity about their rights, duties and responsibilities, their self-efficacy makes them autonomous. They are committed to their new managerial role and they not perceive the administrative activities as a barrier. Nevertheless, the fulfillment of the administrative tasks is considered as one of the main time wasting activities and physicians declare they prioritize clinical activities devolving more time to them than to the administrative ones.

Results indicate that physicians are positively assuming their new double role. However, hospital CEOs should pay more attention to clearly define the rules, the authority and the available resources in order to be helpful to physicians.

By exploring the external side of negotiation, the surveyed physicians appear balanced with respect to their negotiating traits. Through their answers emerges substantial and unaware neutrality with regards to passivity, aggressiveness, arrogance, distress and fatalism during the negotiating processes. This is far from being a positive result. The negotiator's awareness of one or many specific traits leads to the avoidance of a disadvantageous behavior. For example, if a person is aware of being passive during the negotiating processes, he/she can make an effort during the arduous situations without escaping from them. Furthermore, the awareness of being endowed with aggressiveness may drive someone to be open to criticism instead of assuming nervous behavior. The results indicate the need for physicians to deeply explore their negotiating traits even by attending negotiating courses or through the help of life coaches.

Although evidence concerns a small sample of physicians, the empirical approach employed in this chapter can be used to obtain an exhaustive scenario of the double side of negotiation. It makes our results useful for the hospitals CEOs, and for the physicians, helping them to become aware of this challenge.

References

[1] Kreitner, Robert, and Angelo Kinicki. 2004. *Organizational Behavior*, 6th edition, Mc Graw Hill Companies.

[2] Rumiati Rino, and Davide Pietroni. 2001. *La negoziazione*. Raffaello Cortina Editore. (in Italian).

[3] Harvard Business Essential. 2003. *Negotiation*. Harvard business school press, Boston Massachusetts.

[4] Ury, William. 1991. *Getting past no*. Bantam Books.

[5] Pruitt, Dean G., and Peter J. Carnevale. 1993. *Negotiation in social conflict.* Buckingham England, Open University Press.

[6] Weingart, Laurie R., Leigh L. Thomspon, Max Bazerman, and John Carroll. 1990. "Tactical behavior and negotiation outcomes." *International journal of conflict management,* 1: 7-31.

[7] Burgess Heidi, and Guy M. Burgess. 1997. *Encyclopedia of Conflict Resolution.* ABC-CLIO, Denver.

[8] Hood Christopher. 1995. "The " New Public Management" in the 1980s: variation on a theme." *Accounting, organization and society,* 20 (2-3): 93-190.

[9] Christensen Tom, and Peter Lagreid. 2007. *Transcending the new public management. The transformation of public sector reforms*. Ashgate Publishing.

[10] Power Michael. 1997. *The audit society*. Oxford university press, Oxford.
[11] Blomgren Maria. 2003. "Ordering a profession: Swedish nurses encounter new public management reforms." *Financial accounting and management,* 19 (1).
[12] Pollitt, Christopher. 1990. *Managerialism and the public services: The Anglo-American experience*. Oxford: Blackwell.
[13] Ashburner, Lynn. 1994. "The Composition of NHS Trust Boards: A National Perspective." In *NHS Trusts*, edited by Edward Peck and Peter Spurgeon, Longmans, London.
[14] Kitchener, Martin, 2000. "The "Bureaucratization" of professional roles, the case of clinical directors in UK Hospitals." *Organizations,* 7 (1): 129-54.
[15] Kurunmäki, Liisa. 1999. "Professional versus financial capital in the field of healthcare. Struggles for the redistribution of power and control." *Accounting, organization and society,* 24 (2): 95-124.
[16] Kippist Louise, and Anneke Fitzgerald, 2009. "Organizational professional conflict and hybrid clinician managers." *Journal of health organization and management,* 23, 6: 642-655.
[17] Dawson, Sandra, Veronica Mole, Diana Winstanley, and Jim Sherval. 1995. "Management, competition and professional practice: medicine and the marketplace." *British journal of management,* 6: 169-181.
[18] Harrison, Rosemary, and Susan Miller. 1999. "The contribution of clinical directors to the strategic capability of the organization." *British journal of management,* 10: 23-39.
[19] Llewellyn, Sue. 2001. "Two way windows: clinicians as medical managers." *Organization studies,* 22 (4): 593-623.
[20] Rizzo, John R., Robert T. House, and Sidney I. Lirtzman. 1970. "Role conflict and ambiguity in complex organizations." *Administrative science quarterly,* 15 (2): 150-163.
[21] Tengelin, Ellinor, Rebecka Arman, Ewa Wikstrom, and Lotta Dellve. 2011. "Regulating time commitments in healthcare organizations." *Journal of Health organization and management,* 25 (2): 578-599.
[22] Doolin Bill. 2002. "Enterprise discourse, professional identity and the organizational control of hospital clinicians." *Organization studies,* 23 (3): 369-390.
[23] Ferlie, Ewan, Lynn Ashburner, Louise Fitzgerald, and Andrew Pettigrew. 1996. *The new public management in action*. Oxford: Oxford university press.

[24] Causer Gordon, and Mark Exworthy. 1999. "Professionals as managers across the public sector." In *Professionals and the new managerialism in the public sector*, edited by Mark Exworthy and Susan Halford: 83-101. Buckingham England, Open University Press.

[25] Fisher, Joseph G., James R. Frederickson and Sean A. Peffer. 2000. "An experimental investigation of the effects of negotiation." *The accounting review,* 75 (1): 93-114.

[26] Fisher, Joseph G., James R. Frederickson and Sean A. Peffer. 2006. "Budget negotiation in multi- period settings." *Accounting, organization and society,* 31: 511-528.

[27] Arnold Markus C. 2015. "The effect of superiors' exogenous constraints on budget negotiations." *The accounting review,* 90 (1): 31-57.

[28] Morandi Roberto. 2012. *Affacciarsi alla negoziazione. Strumenti pratici per avviare e gestire con successo ogni tipo di trattativa. MRM Communication Edition* (in Italian).

About the Author

Federica Morandi
Department of Management
Catholic University of Sacred Heart
Rome, Italy

INDEX

C

D

E

F

G

H

I

J

L

O

P

Q

R

S

Y